You, Your Relationship & Your ADD

A WORKBOOK

MICHAEL T. BELL, ED.S., LPC, NCC

New Harbinger Publications, Inc.

Publisher's Note

This publication is designed to provide accurate and authoritative information in regard to the subject matter covered. It is sold with the understanding that the publisher is not engaged in rendering psychological, financial, legal, or other professional services. If expert assistance or counseling is needed, the services of a competent professional should be sought.

Distributed in the U.S.A. by Publishers Group West; in Canada by Raincoast Books; in Great Britain by Airlift Book Company, Ltd.; in South Africa by Real Books, Ltd.; in Australia by Boobook; and in New Zealand by Tandem Press.

Cover design by Blue Designs
Edited by Brady Kahn
Text design by Tracy Powell-Carlson

ISBN 1-57224-299-X Paperback

New Harbinger Publications' Web site address: www.newharbinger.com

04   03   02

10   9   8   7   6   5   4   3   2   1

First printing

Thanks to my wife, who stood by me even when I had not yet learned the lessons that are laid out in this book. She is my love and my inspiration.

Thanks to my mother, who fought to get me through my first twelve years of school with love, patience, dedication, and a willingness to fight with the school system to make sure I got the help I needed.

Thanks to Tesilya Hanauer, who recognized that this book was worthy of publication, and to Heather Mitchener and Brady Kahn, who helped me organize my thoughts and ideas in a way that would make sense to you.

Contents

Introduction

ADD is a condition that can impact every area of your life. It can affect your career choices, your sense of self-worth and self-efficacy, your opportunities, and, yes, your relationships. This workbook is not designed to explain ADD or to address every area of your life that ADD affects. Rather, the point is to look at the positive and negative effect of ADD on relationships and to give you some practical suggestions on how to have a healthier and more fulfilling romantic life.

My understanding about ADD comes from firsthand as well as professional experience. I am a licensed professional counselor in private practice in a community about thirty minutes outside of Washington, D.C. I do both individual and couples counseling, and approximately half of the patients I see are children or adults with ADD. In addition to this, I have ADD myself. I know that ADD can make life hard. I also know that if you commit to making changes, even when it does not feel good, that you can do it. You will find that I do not do a great deal of hand-holding. I try to give you recommendations in a relatively brief and straightforward manner. If you are like many adults with ADD, reading thick books is not one of your greatest strengths. Because of this, I made a sincere effort to remove as much fluff as possible and just give you the most helpful information.

Since ADD is a syndrome, not everyone with ADD has exactly the same symptoms. Because of this, not everything in this workbook will apply to you. Chapter 1 includes a quick survey of what follows so that you can give special attention to those chapters that are most relevant to you. Go to those chapters first. You might decide to skim other chapters that are less relevant. I want you to get everything you can from this workbook, so I don't want you wasting your creative energy on parts that are not useful. You don't have to fill in every exercise, but do take the time to complete exercises in sections that relate significantly to you.

There is one thing I would like to clear up before continuing. Some people use the term attention deficit/hyperactivity disorder (ADHD), whereas others use the term attention deficit disorder (ADD). These terms are just different names for the same syndrome. ADD is the older term, but it is still the one most widely used by laypeople, so it is the term I use with the greatest frequency. Don't get too caught up in the terminology. Just ask yourself if a given suggestion is beneficial. If it is, then use it. If not, then skip to the next section. Do take the time, however, to complete the first chapter. I believe it will be useful to everyone using this book.

Chapter 1

Getting All You Can from This Book

By the time you reach adulthood, the social, educational, and personal consequences of being impulsive, hyperactive, and forgetful can take a major toll on your sense of self-worth and self-efficacy. This can set you up for selling yourself short in all areas of your life, including your relationships. You might not feel confident enough to ask people out. You also might inadvertently allow some of your ADD symptoms to sabotage your opportunities for a happy and healthy relationship.

You will probably notice that avoidance is one of the major themes in this workbook. I discuss how people with ADD tend to avoid things that are not exciting and stimulating. Avoidance plays out in the issue of "taking chances" as well. Instead of avoiding something that you do not like or that is not stimulating, you may avoid taking the chance of sticking with something—or doing something new at all—to avoid feeling like a failure. After all, we were probably all too familiar with that feeling as we grew up.

Learn to Take Chances

Following many of the recommendations in this workbook involves taking a risk. It can be anxiety-provoking to think about stepping out of old patterns and trying something new. It may mean taking greater responsibility for yourself and your relationships.

What I am asking you to do is to believe in your ability to make changes. It is often easier to accept that "this is just the way I am" than it is to make changes.

Do you say to yourself something like, "I am just ADD and the rest of the world needs to understand that!" If so, then what you are doing is staying in a safe shell, rather than taking the chance of owning your own life and the impact of your ADD on your relationships. You are simply blaming problems on your neurological makeup so that you don't have to face possible failure. I am asking you to be brave and take a chance.

Get Rid of Limiting Beliefs Right from the Start

Limiting beliefs are defined as the stories we tell ourselves which cause us to sabotage our best efforts (Hartmann 1998). Limiting beliefs often sound something like:

- "I can't do that . . . because . . ."

- "If I . . . then . . ."

- "I don't . . . because . . ."

- "I'm not . . . because . . ."

Actual examples of limiting beliefs that I have heard from individuals with ADD have included statements like:

- "I can't succeed because of my ADD."

- "I would be a success if others did not hold me back."

- "I don't keep a schedule because I don't like to have restrictions on my time."

- "That is just the way I am."

- "If others would back off, then I would be okay."

- "I don't have time to, because there is so much else going on in my life."

- "It's not my fault! If he would just accept me as I am and quit trying to change me then things would be all right."

Limiting beliefs have several functions. They make excuses for us not to change or take personal responsibility for our lives or our relationships. They allow us to blame others, including our romantic partner, for our problems so that we do not have to be personally accountable. They also keep us stuck in life situations and behavioral patterns that set us up for failure and disappointment time and again.

Exercise 1.1

Think of five limiting beliefs, or excuses, that could keep you from making positive changes in your life and relationship(s) after reading this workbook. Write them below and then make an agreement with yourself not to use them.

1. _____

2. _____

3. _____

4. _____

5. _____

✳ ✳ ✳ ✳ ✳

Develop Positive Goals for the Future

I don't know who originally said it, but one of my favorite sayings is, "If you aim for nothing, you are sure to hit it." With that in mind, let us take the time to establish your goals for what you would like to get out of this workbook. Listed below are brief descriptions of each chapter. Read each description. If you are currently in a relationship, you will also want to have your partner read along with you. By understanding what this workbook has to offer in each chapter you will be: better able to decide what your goals are in reading this book, and be better able to focus your energy on those sections that have most relevance to you. By having your romantic partner participate, you are inviting him or her to point out blind spots you might not be aware of. In fact, if you are willing to get your partner's open and honest opinion, without getting defensive, the exercise of surveying the workbook could open up some productive discussions between the two of you.

Exercise 1.2

You will notice a rating scale for many of the chapters that follow. I want you to rate each chapter on how helpful you think that chapter will be for you. Circle the appropriate number on the scale of 1 to 5, in which 1 means "unnecessary" and 5 means "vital to read." If your partner is participating, have him or her rate you on each of these chapters as well.

ADD adults also have a tendency to jump into tasks without first considering the best way to approach them. By taking a quick survey of this workbook with your romantic partner, you will be aware of what is most relevant to you and, thus, make the best use of your time and energy. You will be able to go directly to the chapters that are most important to you first and then address other chapters that are less relevant later on.

Note: I've also included summaries for those chapters that I believe are vital for everyone to read. In these cases, I have omitted the rating scale.

Chapter 2: Assessment and Treatment Issues

This chapter is primarily written for individuals who have not been professionally assessed for ADD. It describes the symptoms of ADD, what conditions can mimic symptoms of ADD, and what conditions can coexist with ADD. Its primary goal is to help the reader become a better-informed consumer of services. This chapter would be:

Rating of Self:

1	2	3	4	5
Unnecessary	Mildly helpful	Helpful	Very Helpful	Vital

Rating by Romantic Partner:

1	2	3	4	5
Unnecessary	Mildly helpful	Helpful	Very Helpful	Vital

Chapter 3: The Positive Side of ADD

This chapter looks at many of the positive characteristics that many adults with ADD bring to relationships. It can be helpful to see ADD in a more positive light. Many of us have several wonderful things that we bring to relationships that make us good romantic partners. This chapter would be:

Rating of Self:

1	2	3	4	5
Unnecessary	Mildly helpful	Helpful	Very Helpful	Vital

Rating by Romantic Partner:

1	2	3	4	5
Unnecessary	Mildly helpful	Helpful	Very Helpful	Vital

Chapter 4: Correcting Incorrect Thinking

This chapter will be helpful if you tend to question your ability to make positive changes in your life, question your sense of self-worth, or become anxious, angry, depressed, or irritable. It will also help you if you tend to focus on how you have been treated unfairly or have difficulty letting go of the past. This chapter would be:

Rating of Self:

1	2	3	4	5
Unnecessary	Mildly helpful	Helpful	Very Helpful	Vital

Rating by Romantic Partner:

1	2	3	4	5
Unnecessary	Mildly helpful	Helpful	Very Helpful	Vital

Chapter 5: Sensitive Spots

This chapter will help you understand how the reactions of others to your ADD during your childhood can still affect you and your relationships today. It also gives exercises to help you deal with your sensitive spots so that they do not continue to negatively impact you and your romantic life. This chapter is important for every adult with ADD to read.

Chapter 6: Avoidance

Avoidance of things that are not stimulating or that require extended concentration and focus is one of the hallmarks of ADD. This chapter helps you identify the harm this tendency has on you and your romantic life and helps you reduce its negative impact. This chapter is important for every adult with ADD to read.

Chapter 7: ADD, Stimulation, and Romantic Relationships

You should read this chapter if you tend to focus on your interests to the detriment of your relationships, if you have a tendency to become bored with your relationships, or if you allow your craving for stimulation to cause you to lose sight of how your behavior is impacting those around you. This chapter would be:

Rating of Self:

1	2	3	4	5
Unnecessary	Mildly helpful	Helpful	Very Helpful	Vital

Rating by Romantic Partner:

1	2	3	4	5
Unnecessary	Mildly helpful	Helpful	Very Helpful	Vital

Chapter 8: Getting Rid of "Frustrations"

This chapter helps you identify those things that are a repeated annoyance or irritation in your life, identify how those frustrations negatively impact you and your romantic life, and reduce or get rid of your frustrations. It also helps you identify those things that you do that are frustrating for your romantic partner and reduce and eliminate them as well. This chapter is important for every adult with ADD to read.

Chapter 9: Better Living through Organization

If you are disorganized and your disorganization causes stress in your life and/or negatively impacts your relationship, then this would be a useful chapter. This chapter would be:

Rating of Self:

1	2	3	4	5
Unnecessary	Mildly helpful	Helpful	Very Helpful	Vital

Rating by Romantic Partner:

1	2	3	4	5
Unnecessary	Mildly helpful	Helpful	Very Helpful	Vital

Chapter 10: Sharing Responsibilities

Do you or your partner have issues over the way duties are divided up in the home? If you do, then I would strongly recommend this chapter. This chapter would be:

Rating of Self:

1	2	3	4	5
Unnecessary	Mildly helpful	Helpful	Very Helpful	Vital

Rating by Romantic Partner:

1	2	3	4	5
Unnecessary	Mildly helpful	Helpful	Very Helpful	Vital

Chapter 11: Learning How to Relax

Read this chapter if you tend to feel physically tense and/or anxious or irritable much of the time. This chapter would be:

Rating of Self:

1	2	3	4	5
Unnecessary	Mildly helpful	Helpful	Very Helpful	Vital

Rating by Romantic Partner:

1	2	3	4	5
Unnecessary	Mildly helpful	Helpful	Very Helpful	Vital

Chapter 12: Dealing with Sarcasm and Anger

This chapter looks at how sarcasm and anger can create problems in your relationship. If you, or your partner, sees anger management or sarcasm as an issue for you, then this would be a good chapter to read. This chapter would be:

Rating of Self:

1	2	3	4	5
Unnecessary	Mildly helpful	Helpful	Very Helpful	Vital

Rating by Romantic Partner:

1	2	3	4	5
Unnecessary	Mildly helpful	Helpful	Very Helpful	Vital

Chapter 13: The Impact of Listening

ADD can clearly impact a person's ability to concentrate, focus, and pay attention. Because of this, your ability to truly listen to your partner can be damaged. This chapter is important for every adult with ADD to read.

Chapter 14: ADD and Sexual Intimacy

This chapter is important for every adult with ADD to read. It discusses how ADD can impact sexual intimacy and what to do to increase sexual intimacy. Exercises are given that would be good for every couple to go through, no matter how good their sex life may be.

Chapter 15: Social Blunders, Poor Boundaries, and Impulsiveness

If you tend to do things in public situations that cause you or your partner to be embarrassed or uncomfortable, then this chapter should be helpful. There is also a section in this chapter that addresses impulsiveness and money issues as well. This chapter would be:

Rating of Self:

1	2	3	4	5
Unnecessary	Mildly helpful	Helpful	Very Helpful	Vital

Rating by Romantic Partner:

1	2	3	4	5
Unnecessary	Mildly helpful	Helpful	Very Helpful	Vital

Chapter 16: The Love Bank

This chapter uses the concept of the love bank to show how emotional withdrawals and investments in a relationship are made. It shows how ADD can set you up for having more emotional withdrawals than investments, which can lead to an emotionally bankrupt relationship. This chapter also shows you how to increase your emotional investments and decrease your emotional withdrawal so that your relationship can be emotionally sound. It is important for every adult with ADD to read.

Chapter 17: ADD and Medications

This chapter looks at the various medications that can be helpful in treating ADHD. This chapter would be:

Rating of Self:

1	2	3	4	5
Unnecessary	Mildly helpful	Helpful	Very Helpful	Vital

Rating by Romantic Partner:

1	2	3	4	5
Unnecessary	Mildly helpful	Helpful	Very Helpful	Vital

Chapter 18: Wrapping Up

Everyone should read this chapter. I would suggest that you first read those chapters you rated a 5, then read those you rated a 4, and so on. Then read this chapter last.

✳ ✳ ✳ ✳ ✳

Exercise 1.3

Now that you and your romantic partner have rated each chapter, set some goals for yourself. Complete the following statements in the space provided.

1. "When I have finished this book I will observe the following positive changes in myself and in my relationships . . ."

_____

_____

_____

_____

2. "I will know that these changes have occurred because I will be able to observe the following changes in my behavior . . ."

_____

_____

_____

_____

3. "I will know these changes have occurred because my significant other will have noticed the following changes in my behavior . . ."

_____

_____

_____

_____

* * * * *

Chapter 2

Assessment and Treatment Issues

The clinical definition for attention deficit disorder is provided in the most recent edition of the *Diagnostic and Statistical Manual of Mental Disorders (DSM-IV-TR)* (APA 2000). The *DSM-IV* uses the term attention deficit hyperactivity disorder, and breaks ADHD down into three subtypes: predominantly *hyperactive-impulsive type*; predominantly *inattentive type*; and *combined type* (meeting the criteria for both the hyperactive-impulsive and inattentive subtypes) (APA 2000).

In the previous edition of the *Diagnostic and Statistical Manual of Mental Disorders*, ADHD was called attention deficit disorder (ADD) and it was broken down into two subtypes, ADD with hyperactivity and ADD without hyperactivity. Simply stated, ADD and ADHD are the same condition. ADD is the classical term and ADHD is the newer term. For the list of *DSM-IV-TR* criteria for ADHD, see appendix A. I do not want to discuss the *DSM-IV* criteria, in depth, however, because they are geared much more toward children than adults. For example, the list of symptoms includes running about or climbing excessively, and having difficulty playing or engaging in leisure activities quietly. The description obviously does not apply to adults.

Assessment of Symptoms

I want to point out that the symptoms of ADD are only the by-product of an underlying neurological condition. ADD is not really an attention problem or a hyperactivity problem. That is only the behavior we see. What we are really dealing with is a neurological *under*stimulation disorder. Show me the typical child with ADD and I will show you a child who can sit down in front of a video game for hours on end. The child with ADD has no trouble concentrating and focusing when there is enough outward stimulation to compensate for his or her neurological understimulation.

Experts agree that you cannot get ADD as an adult. It has to have been present from a very young age. To further complicate matters, often many adult patients were not diagnosed as children because ADD was not widely recognized by health care providers until the late 1960s or early 1970s.

Before assuming you have ADD as an adult, you should speak with a professional trained in the diagnosis and treatment of adults with ADD. The first thing that a professional would need to do is determine your psychiatric status as a child and make a retroactive diagnosis.

If you are being assessed, your doctor or therapist should preferably speak with your parents to determine if you exhibited symptoms of ADD in childhood. If your parent or parents cannot be spoken to directly, then it would be good to have one of them complete an ADD questionnaire. If neither parent is available, you will have to rely on your own memory. (Note: Usually a parent's memory of a patient's childhood behavior at home and at school is more reliable than that of a patient. After all, as a child you had not yet developed the adequate cognitive and emotional skills necessary to observe yourself. Your parents, however, were supposedly responsible for observing your behavior and helping you to become a functional adult, so they would have been more likely to be aware of those things—such as your difficultly completing tasks or staying focused or making friends—that would have gotten in the way of you becoming a functional adult. I see children all the time who say that they have no trouble paying attention in class, but their teacher might be sending home letters to the parents every week stating that they are having trouble paying attention. As a result, when they become adults it will be their parents who have the better recollection of their behavior.)

After a childhood history of symptoms related to ADD is confirmed, then it is important to establish that symptoms have been consistent through adulthood. It important to note that, while adult ADD symptoms worsen when an ADD adult is under stress, they are present with the adult even in the absence of a stress-producing situation.

If you wish to get a quick look at the possibility of whether you have ADD or not, then I would suggest using an online test called the "Amen Clinic Adult ADD Test." This online test was created by Dr. Daniel Amen. He is a true pioneer in the field of ADD. His test has seventy-six items for rating yourself. After you have rated yourself on all seventy-six items, you can submit your test for results to determine whether or not ADD is a possibility. If you would like to go online and take this test, then you can go to his Web site (see appendix D). I would strongly suggest that, instead of just rating yourself, you ask someone else to rate you as well. Choose someone who knows you very well such as a close friend, a long-time business partner, or your spouse. People often have difficulty observing themselves in any kind of objective manner. Having someone else rate you will help make sure that you are not missing important information due to blind spots.

Adult ADD Symptoms

Below is a list of symptoms for adult ADD which I have made based on various readings and clinical observations. Because ADD is a syndrome, certain symptoms may be descriptive of you and others may not. If you do have ADD, however, a great many of these symptoms will sound familiar.

- distractibility

- difficulty paying attention to what others are saying (thoughts tend to wander)

- difficulty concentrating when reading

- tendency to not finish what you start, to leave several projects undone

- tendency to seek caretakers to manage the details of life that you find overwhelming

- difficulty staying focused during intense learning situations

- disorganization

- difficulty planning things out in a step-by-step sequence

- difficulty with details (such as paperwork)

- resistance to tasks that require sustained mental effort (particularly tasks that are not interesting or stimulating), and tendency to procrastinate on such tasks

- tendency to lose or misplace things

- chronic forgetfulness

- tendency to manage time poorly

- tendency to take on too many tasks and then feel overwhelmed

- tendency to feel like an underachiever in life

- subject to periodic depression

- tendency toward addiction (work, alcohol, drugs, etc.)

- tendency to feel late, rushed, or unprepared

- chronic feelings of tension or nervousness (frequently present even when there is not anything particular to feel anxious about)

- trouble going to sleep at night and trouble getting up in the morning

- tendency to become irritated

- subject to frequent job changes

- subject to frequent moves

- tendency to jump from hobby to hobby or interest to interest

- tendency to manage finances poorly and spend money impulsively

- difficulty controlling temper

- tendency to speak without thinking

- tendency to feel restless

- "nervous habits" such as tapping or drumming of fingers
- tendency to be talkative
- tendency to have poor physical boundaries
- tendency to intrude on or interrupt others
- difficulty waiting your turn in interactions with others
- tendency to give a response before someone has finished a question
- difficulty maintaining long-term relationships

For such symptoms to be truly indicative of adult ADD, then the following should also be true:

1. Problems with hyperactivity and/or inattention must have been present before you were seven years of age.

2. The symptoms need to be more noticeable than in the average adult.

3. The symptoms must be observed in more than just one area of your life. For instance, your symptoms would need to have an impact at home and at work.

4. The symptoms must interfere with your academic, social, or occupational functioning.

5. The symptoms can't be better explained by another medical and/or mental health condition.

Who Should Diagnose You?

There are various opinions on who is best qualified to assess adults for ADD. In their book *Adult ADD: The Complete Handbook*, doctors David Sudderth and Joseph Kandel state, "Because we believe that ADD is a neurologic disease, we also think that ADD is best diagnosed by a neurologist, particularly one interested in cognitive neurology" (1997, 69).

I do not happen to think that it is necessary to schedule an appointment with a neurologist to be properly assessed for ADD. In my opinion, a professional's familiarity with the diagnosis and treatment of ADD adults is most important. Any of the following types of professionals, with the proper training and experience, would be qualified to diagnose and treat ADD:

- neurologists
- psychiatrists
- clinical psychologists
- licensed professional counselors
- licensed clinical social workers
- certified nurse specialists

Note that only medical doctors, such as neurologists and psychiatrists, can prescribe medication for ADD.

Finding a Qualified Professional

When interviewing someone, it is always a good idea to have the questions that you want to ask prepared ahead of time and to write down the responses so that you do not forget. Appendix B includes a questionnaire which you should feel free to use when interviewing professionals. It contains spaces to fill in the responses of each professional you interview.

Don't be surprised if it is difficult to find someone who knows a great deal about treating adult ADD. You might want to check with a local Children and Adults with Attention Deficit Disorder (CHADD) group to see if they might have any referrals so that you can shorten your search. Regional CHADD groups can be found by going on CHADD's Web site (see appendix D). It is worth taking the time to find someone who really knows how to assess and treat adults with ADD. Even though this might be a little bit more of a hassle on the front end, it will keep you from wasting time and money later on, and risking less than adequate treatment.

What Next?

After you have decided on a treatment provider, I would recommend doing some of the doctor's work ahead of time:

1. Lay out your family history. Have your mother and/or father complete the questions for the parent and family questionnaire located in appendix C and take the results to your appointment.

2. Go to Dr. Amen's Web site (see appendix D) and complete both the adult test and the subtype test. Print out both the questions and the results and take these to your appointment.

3. Have someone in your personal life who knows you very well complete the adult test for you as well. Have him or her fill it out without you being in the room. You want an independent evaluation of your behavior. Once your friend has completed the questionnaire, take these results with you to your appointment as well.

4. If possible, have a professional colleague with whom you work closely complete the adult test for you too. (Once again, have the person fill it out without your being in the room.) It will help if your treatment provider can see the impact of symptoms in both your personal and professional life.

5. Have the names and dosages of any medications you are currently on written down ahead of time so that you will have this information readily available.

6. Be able to clearly express what is bringing you into treatment and what your hopes for treatment are. Be able to state your hopes for treatment in clear behavioral terms. To help you clarify your goals, answer the following questions:

- "If I entered treatment, I would know that treatment was a success if I noticed what changes?" _____

  _____

  _____

  _____

- "Others would be able to observe what kind of changes in me?" _____

  _____

  _____

  _____

Taking the above steps will facilitate communication with your treatment provider. He or she will be better able to understand your symptoms and history, and grasp them more quickly. The treatment provider will be better able to understand what you want to get out of treatment. As a result, you will be able to see a positive response to treatment sooner.

Differential Diagnosis and Comorbid Conditions

When considering if a person has ADD or not, it is important to consider if the symptoms present could be better explained by another medical or mental health condition. When I talk about "differential diagnosis," I am talking about differentiating ADD from another condition that may mimic many of the symptoms of ADD. For instance, anxiety and ADD have very different causes for similar symptoms. Even though the symptoms may appear very much the same, the modes of treatment for each would be different. Because of this, it is important to differentiate between an anxiety disorder and ADD.

When I talk about comorbid conditions, I am talking about conditions that occur at the same time. For instance, it is certainly possible that an individual could have both ADD and an anxiety disorder. Proper diagnosis and care requires that practitioners consider conditions that have a greater likelihood of occurring with ADD.

Depression

There is certainly a higher rate of depression among individuals with ADD than in the general population. Research has also shown that there is a higher rate of relatives with depression among individuals with ADD than in the general population.

One theory of depression supports the contention that depression is learned helplessness. In my own work with adults and children with ADD, I see time and again how the symptoms of ADD can have a devastating impact on my patients' sense of self-efficacy, or ability to have power and control in their own lives. They experience both the negative impact of degrading statements from others and the continued emotional erosion caused by the symptoms throughout their lives. These negative statements and experiences can be internalized, which can certainly help set up an individual for depression. Individuals with depression, ADD, or both need to do the following in treatment:

1. Identify and replace negative self-statements.

2. Identify areas of competence in their lives and expand those competencies.

3. Learn ways to challenge beliefs that question their lack of competence and lack of control.

4. Be evaluated by a physician to determine the need for medications.

Anxiety

As someone who specializes in the treatment of adults with ADD, I can say that it is not always clear right off the bat if an individual has ADD or generalized anxiety, or both. Anxiety and ADD share many of the same symptoms. To make diagnosis even more complicated, most individuals with ADD have some elevated degree of anxiety due to their ADD. There is no doubt that ADD makes life more stressful due to your forgetfulness, difficulty concentrating, speaking without thinking, and so on. Also, many adults with ADD show a general overreaction to stressors and are angered and irritated easily.

While it often takes a well-trained professional to distinguish clearly between a primary diagnosis of ADD and a primary diagnosis of generalized anxiety, it is very important to do so. If a misdiagnosis of ADD is made, many of the neurostimulant medications will only exacerbate the anxiety condition. If a misdiagnosis of generalized anxiety is made, then the medications may be somewhat helpful, but they often will not have near the efficacy as a neurostimulant medication. I remember a case only a year or two ago when I had an individual who I strongly felt had a primary diagnosis of ADD. I felt his anxiety symptoms were a secondary reaction to his ADD. His family doctor refused to place him on a neurostimulant, and instead placed him on an SSRI (e.g., Paxil, Prozac) and then tried him on Wellbutrin. Both medications resulted in little to no improvement. My patient was highly discouraged. I finally convinced the doctor to prescribe a one-week trial of Adderall (a type of neurostimulant) to see what the results would be. He reluctantly agreed, and the results were remarkable. My patient showed a dramatic reduction in his level of anxiety and irritability. His organization improved, and he made marked progress in treatment.

Whether you have ADD, generalized anxiety, or both, it is important to:

1. Learn to reduce overreactions to life events

2. Learn body-based relaxation techniques

3. Learn to reduce stressors and frustrations in your life

4. Learn to avoid avoidance

5. Exchange beliefs that contribute to anxiety for more rational beliefs

6. Be evaluated by a physician to determine the need for medications

Post-Traumatic Stress Disorder

While I am not aware of any research that supports a higher rate of post-traumatic stress disorder (PTSD) among adults with ADD than in the general population, it is important to note that a differential diagnosis needs to be made between ADD and PTSD. PTSD and ADD share some of the same symptoms including avoidance, difficulty with concentration, and poor academic or work performance. There are some clear differences, however, between ADD and PTSD. PTSD occurs after a severe traumatic experience. Examples of the type of events that could cause PTSD would include an assault (either physical and/or sexual) or participation in combat. Individuals with PTSD (and not ADD) often do not have a history of impulsive/hyperactive behavior and inattention. Their symptoms would have become present only after experiencing the traumatic event. Individuals with PTSD also have flashbacks, which are not present in individuals who have ADD (but not PTSD).

Substance Abuse

Conservative estimates hold that between 0.5 percent and 5 percent of adults in the United States display at least residual signs of ADD. Among individuals seeking treatment for substance abuse, however, between 10 percent to 20 percent of those individuals meet the criteria for ADD. Many professionals believe that cocaine, alcohol, and other substances are used by individuals with ADD to self-medicate. However, contrary to the concerns of some professionals, there is evidence that the proper use of neurostimulant medication might even decrease the likelihood of the abuse of substances (Levin 2000).

Learning Disabilities

Adults with ADD are much more likely than others to have a learning disability. This often compounds a feeling of inadequacy.

Other Mental Health Conditions

Research has also shown that there is a higher likelihood for individuals with ADD to have obsessive-compulsive disorder (OCD) and Tourette's syndrome.

Neurological and Medical Conditions That Can Mimic ADD

Sudderth and Kandel (1997) point to the following neurological and medical problems that can mimic ADD symptoms:

- frontal lobe disease

- epilepsy

- acquired immune deficiency syndrome (AIDS)

- Lyme disease

- thyroid disease

It is important to remember that ADD is a condition that starts in childhood. If you did not have symptoms of ADD in childhood, then it is probably safe to assume that there is a better explanation for your symptoms now than ADD. If there are noticeable changes in your ability to concentrate and focus, your activity level, your impulsivity, your irritability level, or your personality that persist for any length of time and that are not clearly related to significant stressors in your life, then it is a good idea to have a complete medical evaluation. Even if you do feel that ADD is a strong possibility, you should discuss your concerns with your family doctor and have a complete physical. I have learned from my experience as a therapist that physical conditions such as hormonal imbalances, Lyme disease, and brain tumors can all be mistaken for mental health conditions. It is always a good idea to have a complete physical as part of any kind of mental health assessment.

Chapter 3

The Positive Side of ADD

It is important for you to be fully aware of your strengths if you are to make the best use of them. The exercises in this chapter will help you identify positive characteristics about yourself so that you can increase their positive impact on your romantic relationship and keep your strengths from becoming liabilities. By having a greater awareness of your strengths, such as humor, creativity, willingness to take risks, lack of inhibition, ability to focus, loyalty, and tenacity, you will be better able to use them.

Humor

If you have ever read the personals in the paper, you know that a whole lot of people want someone who has a sense of humor. Many adults with ADD can have a great sense of humor. Sometimes we need to learn to not say things that are offensive, and we also need to learn when it is important to stop and listen and not joke around. But that does not change the fact that many of us can be a riot at times.

There is no doubt that a sense of humor can have a positive effect on a relationship. Because of a lifetime of dealing with the stress related to your ADD, you may have learned what to take seriously and not to take seriously. You have learned to approach life with a certain amount of lightheartedness as a way to survive. This same skill can also help with the survival of relationships.

As a therapist, I have met several couples who could have used a serious injection of a humor. We all need to learn to laugh at ourselves and the silly situations in which we place ourselves. If we don't, then getting through life is going to be fairly difficult (or at least not much fun).

Exercise 3.1

If you can be a relatively lighthearted person at times, how has your sense of humor had a positive impact on your personal life? How has it helped you in relationships? _____

_____

_____

_____

If you are currently in a relationship, what does your partner like about your sense of humor? _____

_____

_____

What do you need to do to make your sense of humor continue to have a positive influence on your relationship? What do you need to do to keep it from having a negative impact? __

_____

_____

_____

✳ ✳ ✳ ✳ ✳

Creativity

Adults with ADD are often good at "thinking outside of the box." We can often look at the same old situation and come up with new and creative solutions. This can have a positive impact on relationships. Instead of just getting mired down in a problem, we can see alternatives. The problem is that our creative juices often get shut down once we have become angry, upset, or stressed. We do not seem to have the same amount of creativity we have when we can calmly deal with something. However, if we can stay calm in the face of relationship stressors, we have a wonderful wellspring of creativity that we can utilize.

Exercise 3.2

In what ways are you creative? _____

_____

_____

_____

_____

How has this creativity positively impacted your romantic life? _____

_____

_____

_____

How can you better utilize your creativity to increase the positive impact it has on your personal life and to increase your ability to deal with conflicts? Because you are such a creative person, I am giving you twice as much space to answer this question. _____

_____

_____

_____

_____

_____

_____

_____

✳ ✳ ✳ ✳ ✳

Willingness to Take Risks

As Susan Roberts and Gerard Jansen point out in *Living with ADD: A Workbook for Adults with Attention Deficit Disorder*, "The impatience that often accompanies ADD can lead some to take the plunge—ADDers are more likely to try, instead of sitting on the sidelines as the opportunities of life pass them by" (1997, 15).

Risk-taking can have a positive impact on your romantic life simply because starting a new relationship requires taking a risk. That is, nothing ventured, nothing gained.

There are also positive ramifications of risk-taking within the context of relationships. The following story illustrates this. As in this case, all the stories in this workbook come from my personal or professional experiences. Certain details have been changed to maintain the confidentiality of my patients.

Michaela and Tad's Story

Michaela and Tad started out as business partners before they became romantically involved. They were quite an interesting pair. Michaela, the partner with ADD, was highly outgoing and vivacious. She was loaded with good ideas and always ready to tackle something new. While Tad was supportive of Michaela, he was a good grounding force for her in both the business and romantic aspects of their relationship.

If it were not for Michaela, they would have never left their original place of employment and ventured out on their own. She was able to drum up business and develop a marketing strategy that really got their new business off the ground. Tad, on the other hand, was great at the details. He appreciated Michaela's risk-taking and creativity, but was able to point out possible pitfalls so that her risk-taking did not get out of hand. Through some counseling, Michaela was able to see that Tad was not holding her back, but that he was simply trying to make her aware of what could prevent her dreams from happening. She came to value and appreciate this.

Tad, on the other hand, was able to share how he greatly appreciated the extent to which Michaela's risk-taking had broadened his horizons. Before he met her, he had done little traveling and had not tried a great many new things. He recognized that he had been exposed to several things that he never would have tried. This had helped him gain confidence in himself and helped him to enjoy life more.

Exercise 3.3

What positive impact has risk-taking played in your relationship(s)? _____

_____

_____

_____

What things do you need to keep in mind when taking risks? How can you use your romantic partner as a grounding force in your life so that your risk-taking tendencies remain a positive factor in your life? _____

_____

_____

_____

✳ ✳ ✳ ✳ ✳

Lack of Inhibition

While impulsiveness, or lack of inhibition, can have lots of negative consequences within the context of relationships, it can also create lots of positives. It can lead to:

- More fun. Sometimes it can be great to spontaneously start up a snowball fight. A lack of inhibition can also make party games a lot more fun.

- More honesty. While saying what flows off the frontal lobe can hurt the feelings of others, it can also be good for relationships to say what is on your mind instead of "just beating around the bush." Such a tendency can help insure that issues are dealt with in the open and don't go unspoken.

- More sexual freedom. An uninhibited partner who is also sensitive to his or her partner can help to make sex a lot more fun by being uninhibited.

It can also add to the spice of life. An uninhibited person is more likely to try new things. With Tad and Michaela, Tad was greatly able to benefit from Michaela's uninhibited qualities. He even stated jokingly that he felt he would have become a "lonely old hermit" without her. Instead, he learned to enjoy new foods, books, movies, Broadway plays, traveling, and a variety of other things. His people skills also improved

Exercise 3.4

If you would describe yourself as uninhibited, what positive impact has this had on your romanitc life? _____

_____

_____

_____

If you are currently in a relationship, what does your partner like about your ability to be uninhibited? _____

_____

_____

_____

What do you need to do to make your uninhibited nature a continued positive influence in your relationship? What do you need to do to keep it from having a negative impact?

_____

_____

_____

＊ ＊ ＊ ＊ ＊

Ability to Focus

As Roberts and Jansen (1997) state, "Although problems in mustering and maintaining attention are the hallmark of ADD, the ability to focus extremely well for long periods of time characterizes ADD, too. This ability to focus intensely, called *hyperfocusing*, is a state when attention is so specifically focused that almost nothing else exists at that moment." (14)

Later, in chapter 7, we will discuss the negative impact that hyperfocusing can have on relationships, but it is also important to note that hyperfocusing can have a very positive impact, particularly early on when the relationship itself becomes the thing on which the ADD partner hyperfocuses.

For hyperfocusing to have a positive impact after the "honeymoon period" of your relationship, you need to learn to combine your hyperfocusing with your creativity to come up with new ways to continue to make your love feel cared for and important.

For many adults hyperfocusing occurs unconsciously. We don't think about it, we are just automatically drawn to whatever is new or exciting. ADD adults need to learn to become aware of our hyperfocusing tendencies so that we can gain control over hyperfocusing. In this way, hyperfocusing can have a positive, rather than negative, long-term impact on relationships. If you have a tendency to hyperfocus, then answer the following questions below:

Exercise 3.5

What positive impact has hyperfocusing had on your relationships in the past? _____

_____

_____

_____

What do you need to do to gain greater control over your hyperfocusing tendencies to help your hyperfocusing become a long-term positive? _____

_____

_____

_____

* * * * *

Loyalty

Not all, but many, adults with ADD can have a strong sense of loyalty. I personally feel that this stems back to childhood issues. Because making friends was so difficult for us as children and we might have felt picked on or ignored, when we did find someone who liked us and wanted to be around us, we treasured that friendship. We learned to value a good friendship.

In the same way, if we are lucky enough to find someone who values us and accepts us, many of us can be very loyal partners.

Exercise 3.6

How have your childhood experiences led you to value a good friend and/or lover?

_____

_____

_____

If you are currently in a relationship, what do you most value about the way your love treats you? _____

_____

_____

_____

How do these things make you more loyal to your love? _____

_____

_____

_____

✳ ✳ ✳ ✳ ✳

Tenacious

Because adults with ADD have a lifetime of dealing with the adversity that ADD can bring, many of us have developed some real tenacity when it comes to dealing with adverse situations. If we apply our tenaciousness to relationships in a positive way, then we can have the stick-to-itive power to work our way through the rough spots.

Exercise 3.7

What kinds of adversity have you overcome in your own life? _____

_____

_____

_____

What have you learned from these experiences? _____

_____

_____

_____

How do these positive life lessons apply to relationships? How can you use them to help you stay with a relationship that is worth keeping? _____

_____

_____

_____

Chapter 4

Correcting Incorrect Thinking

ADD can lead to various types of irrational beliefs that can get in the way of your love life. Irrational beliefs can cause you to feel paranoid, angry, irritable, hurt, and anxious. A person who displays paranoia, anger, irritability, hurt, or anxiety a great deal of the time can be a hard person to live with.

I want you to be able to look at and replace those irrational thought patterns that contribute to negative feelings and reactions so that you will be more open and ready to have healthy relationships. Think of this chapter as a kind of house cleaning chapter. Its purpose is to help you get rid of the thoughts and attitudes that lead to emotional chaos in your life so that you are better prepared to have a healthy relationship.

Self-Efficacy vs. Self-Esteem

Out of all the beliefs that need to change, the most important one to change first is the belief that you cannot change. This relates to your sense of self-efficacy. Instead of using the term *self-esteem*, I prefer the term *self-efficacy*. While the term self-esteem relates to your sense of self-worth, self-efficacy relates more to your sense of your ability to have control of and enact change in your life. In other words, I do not want you just to feel better about yourself. I want you to see how you have control of your own life and destiny.

From a practical standpoint, self-efficacy and self-esteem sound a lot alike. They both relate to the statements you make about yourself and your abilities. There are several reasons why adults with ADD can have low amounts of both. As a child, you probably remember much of life being a struggle. You might not have liked trouble, but due to disorganization, hyperactivity, and impulsivity, you might have found yourself in trouble a great deal of the time. You probably heard lots of "whys," such as "Why can't you just listen?" or "Why can't you just sit still and behave?" or "Why do I have to keep telling you the same thing over and over again?" The truth was that you did not know why. In all likelihood, you were left with a feeling that there was just something flawed or wrong about you that you could not change, no matter how hard you tried. At some point, you even might have decided to give up trying to change certain things about yourself and just accepted them because that was the easiest thing to do. You sacrificed your sense of self-efficacy to avoid the pain of disappointment and failure.

Internalization of Negative Statements

Unhealthy responses to your romantic partner's behavior can be largely based on your reactions to negative statements that you heard as a child and have internalized. For instance, you might have felt as a child that others assumed you were incompetent. Part of you might feel that this was true, and you carry this sense around with you as an adult. As a result, you might depend on your romantic partner to take care of things. If your partner then asks, "Why can't you take care of things yourself?" You might feel hurt that he or she has confirmed your internalized negative self-statement and respond with anger.

Because your internalized negative self-statements can have such a strong impact on your life and relationships, it is important to be able to identify them so that you can expose, challenge, and replace them with healthier thought patterns. The following two exercises will help you achieve this.

Exercise 4.1

Below are a list of some negative self-statements that adults with ADD might be likely to make about themselves. I would like you to rate yourself on each of these beliefs on a scale of 1 to 10, in which 1 signifies a belief that you do not hold at all and 10 means a strongly held belief that you repeatedly and consistently hold. Circle the appropriate number.

I am so incompetent.	1	2	3	4	5	6	7	8	9	10
I lose everything.	1	2	3	4	5	6	7	8	9	10
I am always late.	1	2	3	4	5	6	7	8	9	10
I am such a slob.	1	2	3	4	5	6	7	8	9	10
I am so forgetful.	1	2	3	4	5	6	7	8	9	10
I am so disorganized.	1	2	3	4	5	6	7	8	9	10
I just can't think before I speak.	1	2	3	4	5	6	7	8	9	10

I'm so stupid.	1	2	3	4	5	6	7	8	9	10
I'm always losing my temper.	1	2	3	4	5	6	7	8	9	10

✳ ✳ ✳ ✳

The above beliefs can destroy your sense of self-efficacy and leave you feeling powerless as an agent for change. They can become almost as strong a part of your identity as your ethnicity or your gender if you allow them to.

It is important for you to change such beliefs about yourself if you are to be an agent of change in your own life and relationships. When you hold certain views about yourself, you may be good at finding information that confirms those views and discounting information that does not. In cognitive-behavioral therapy, this pattern of irrational thinking is termed *filtering*. In other words, you put your experiences through a mental filter, and you filter out information that does not match with your belief. For example, you may say to yourself that you are *always* late because you are running late for a meeting, while you discount the fact that yesterday you got to work on time and picked up the kids for soccer on time. You would be taking the negative details and magnifying them while filtering out positive information.

We generally know we are filtering when we use absolute terms like *never* and *always*, such as if we say that we "never" remember things or that we are "always" late or that we are "always" forgetting things or that we "never" do things right.

Exercise 4.2

Step One

If you rated yourself relatively high on any of the statements in the previous exercise, there is a strong likelihood that you are using filtering as a way of confirming your negative beliefs. What I would like you to do now is to challenge these beliefs by observing times that they do not hold true.

If you rated yourself high on the statements "I am so incompetent" or "I am so stupid," I want you to spend the next week identifying areas in your life and times in your life that you are competent. When do you remember to do what you are supposed to do, and when do you get things done the way they are supposed to be done?

If you believe that you lose everything, I would like for you to identify those times this week that you do keep track of things. I would be willing to bet you are only aware of the times you lose your wallet or keys, not the times you remember them. I would also bet that there are certain things you hardly ever lose, but you don't think about these things because you don't lose them.

If you rated yourself high on the statement "I am always late," I would like for you to spend the next week keeping track of times that you are on time.

If you rated yourself high on the statement "I am so forgetful," I want you to track those times this week that you do remember to do things.

If you rated yourself high on the statement "I am so disorganized," I want you to track areas and times in your life where you have chosen to have order.

If you rated yourself high on the statement "I'm always losing my temper," I want you to identify times this week that you could have gotten angry but did not.

Over the next week identify your negative self-statements and then identify times that they do not hold true. Use the space provided to keep track of exceptions to your negative self-statements. If you need more space, continue the list on a separate piece of paper.

Negative Self-Statement	Times the Negative Self-Statement Does Not Hold True

Step Two

After you have spent a week identifying times that your negative self-statements do not hold true, I would like for you to identify what you are doing differently during those times. This task is often very difficult for people. We are often much better at identifying why something went wrong than analyzing why things went right. When things are going right, we often attribute it to good fortune, but when things go wrong, we tend to blame ourselves. After all, if you have ADD and if something goes wrong, it is a good bet that it is your fault, right?

Whether you realize it or not, you are often responsible for creating your own good fortune. When you do remember to do something that you frequently forget to do, how do you manage that? If there are certain things such as lunch or car keys that you never forget, why is that? If you function very well in certain areas in your life, what is different in these cases, and how can you use this information to cope better in other areas of your life? When you are able to think before you speak, what are you doing differently? When you do handle things in an organized manner, how do you do so? How can you do more of it?

If you are not always messing up in your life, then when you are not messing up, you must be doing something differently. You have developed some healthy habits that can, in some way, be re-created in other areas of your life. Perhaps you are using a method to help you think before you act. Maybe you are using the aid of others or visual prompts to help you remember things. Pay attention to whatever is working for you already.

You can extend the same skills to other areas of your life to expand your scope of competence. You can proceed in a more thoughtful and conscious manner. Over the next week, use the space provided to identify not only times that your negative self-statements do not hold true, but also what you are doing to help create those times.

Negative Self-Statement	When It Does Not Hold True	What You Are Doing Differently

Step Three

This is where we expand on what you've been doing right. Review the list you made in step 2. Take a look at how you decided to do things differently when your negative self-statements were not holding true. Now use the space below to identify ways that you could:

1. Do more of what you are doing right more consistently in its current use and situation.

2. Expand your field of competence by coming up with new and creative ways of doing what you are doing right in other areas of your life.

To help jump-start your brainstorming session, ask yourself the following types of questions:

- What am I doing differently when there are exceptions?

- What is different about the situation when there are exceptions?

- How can I do more of what I am doing right?

_____

_____

_____

_____

_____

_____

Step Four

Brainstorming and having good ideas is not enough. You have to be willing to commit to doing things differently. Review your ideas from step 3. Then in the space provided, write down at least three examples of how you are going to commit to making change:

_____

_____

_____

_____

_____

* * * * *

How Our Thought Patterns Can Defeat Us

Earlier in the chapter, I talked about how the irrational thought process of filtering can have a negative impact on your sense of self-efficacy. This next exercise looks at how other kinds of irrational thought patterns may cause havoc in your life. It also helps you cope with this type of thinking.

Exercise 4.3

In this exercise, you will read some descriptions of irrational thought patterns. After each description, please rate yourself on a scale of 1 to 10; a 1 means that the type of thinking described has little to no impact on your life and a 10 represents an extreme impact on your life. For each type of thinking in which you rate yourself with a 5 or higher, take the time to write down how that irrational thought plays out. Then read the following suggestions on how to deal with this kind of thinking.

Catastrophizing

Catastrophizing is when you assume the worst is going to happen. Many individuals with ADD often feel that the world is going to fall apart. We also tend to be highly imaginative, and we can often do a great job at playing out horrible scenarios in our heads. When we are catastrophizing, we look like we are running around like a chicken with its head cut off, we act highly dependent and helpless, or we shut down in the hopes that someone else (such as our romantic partner) will rescue us. Sometimes we get very angry and upset, tearful and highly emotional, or all of the above. We are not, however, likely to think in a clear and rational manner. These are the times when we are apt to make situations worse for ourselves and our romantic partner instead of improve them.

Self-Rating for Catastrophizing

1   2   3   4   5   6   7   8   9   10

In the space below write down ways that catastrophizing has played out in your life and relationship.

_____

_____

_____

_____

_____

_____

Ways to Deal with Catastrophizing

1. Imagine some possible safe alternatives to the worst-case scenario.

2. Think in terms of percentages. For instance, instead of thinking to yourself, "If I go out on the road, I could get into a car accident and die!" ask yourself, "What is the likelihood of that happening?"

3. Check things out with a trusted friend. Choose someone who will help you tap into your own strengths rather than try to solve the problem for you. Choose someone who is level-headed and who, without judging you, will help you look at the situation in a more rational manner.

4. Often the worst-case scenario might be unpleasant, but it is not horrible. Even if you lost that job, it does not mean that you can't get another one, and even if the other person no longer wants to be your friend, it does not mean that life will not be worth living or that you are unlovable. It is often good to ask if your worst-case scenario would really be a catastrophe. If not, then why catastrophize?

Mind Reading

Mind reading involves making snap decisions or assumptions about what others may be thinking when you really have not checked it out. Many individuals with ADD grew up with a sense of rejection. Because of poor social skills and impulsive behavior as a child, we often may have felt ignored or rejected by peers and criticized by adults. As a result, our first assumption as to what others think may tend to be negative. For instance, you might quickly assume that your romantic partner is thinking lots of negative things about you (for example, that you are stupid or lazy) when he or she is not thinking anything of the kind.

Besides assuming that you are being rejected by others or that others are thinking negative thoughts about you, mind reading can lead to making assumptions that others think and feel the same as you do in the same situation. For instance, you might start talking to your romantic partner about how inappropriate and obnoxious the small child in the restaurant is while your partner might be thinking "what a cute child."

Self-Rating for Mind Reading

1	2	3	4	5	6	7	8	9	10

In the space below write down ways that mind reading plays out in your life and romantic relationships.

_____

_____

_____

_____

_____

Ways to Deal with Mind Reading

1. Instead of assuming what others think, check it out. When I first started doing this, I was surprised to find out how wrong I frequently was in my assumptions about what others thought of me and of other things.

2. Remember that "to assume makes an *ass* of *u* and *me*." Don't assume that others are annoyed by the same things that annoy you, care about the same things that you care about, hold the same political or religious beliefs that you hold, or, in general, think the same way you do. If you do, you will far more frequently find yourself with your foot in your mouth.

Overgeneralization

Overgeneralization involves drawing a conclusion from one experience or event and extending that conclusion to all future experiences or events of like nature. This often means giving up before you even try to do something just because you've had one or more bad experiences. For example, you were turned down for a job promotion in the past, so you do not try again because you assume you will be turned down again. Or, you were rejected by someone in the past, so you do not ask anyone else out on a date because you assume you will be rejected again. Based on past events, you predict all future events.

The tendency to overgeneralize is increased for individuals with ADD because of many of the reasons already discussed. The problem is that we assume that rejection, in whatever form, will come, so we create a self-fulfilling prophecy. We might not be as aggressive or assertive as we need to be to get what we want, and, thus, we don't get it. We might be overly aggressive in dealing with people, including our romantic partner, because we are so used to dealing with rejection that we will automatically assume a defensive stance. What we really do is put others off. However we do it, we can often behave in a way that sets us up for future failure, thus allowing our belief that we will fail to become self-fulfilling.

Self-Rating for Overgeneralization

1   2   3   4   5   6   7   8   9   10

In the space below write down ways that overgeneralization plays out in your life and romantic relationships.

_____

_____

_____

_____

_____

Ways to Deal with Overgeneralization

1. Realize that your future has not been predetermined and that you are responsible for creating your own reality.

2. View your past experiences as lessons to help you determine what to do, or not do, in the future. Instead of seeing yourself as trapped and your future being predetermined, you can begin to view yourself as having gained greater wisdom for dealing with future events. That way, no matter what the outcome, you win. You either get what you want or you gain greater knowledge to help you get what you want in the future.

3. Realize that if you do nothing, you get nothing. If you take a chance, you might not get what you want, but if you don't even try, you are sure not to get what you want. It is kind of like the old joke of the guy who prayed to God every day to help him win the lottery. He finally heard a loud voice from heaven saying, "Buy a ticket, fool!"

4. Ask yourself, "If I were behaving as if I were going to get what I wanted, what would I be doing differently?" After you ask the question, then change your behavior accordingly.

Shoulds

"Shoulds" are ironclad beliefs about how you and other people ought to act. You may often feel resentful and angry at others when they break the "rules" and guilty when you do. The problem with shoulds is that they are expectations. Expectations do not lead to happiness and satisfaction in life. In fact, they only lead to unhappiness and dissatisfaction. These fixed beliefs keep us from appropriately evaluating ourselves and others, based on personal circumstances. We come across and behave as inflexible, cold, angry, and rigid.

Let's take a common example of one such belief. Assume you say to yourself, "People should be more understanding of me because I have ADD." First off, if you think your boss or customer is going to be understanding of you messing up because you have ADD, or your spouse or significant other is going to be more understanding of your insensitivity due to your ADD, then in what world do you live! It would be better if people could be more understanding, but it is just not a reasonable expectation.

If you argue with others a great deal, or others would describe you as bullheaded or highly opinionated, you might want to consider this before you rate yourself. If you are thinking, "I just happen to always be right," think again.

Self-Rating for Shoulds

1   2   3   4   5   6   7   8   9   10

In the space below write down ways that shoulds play out in your life and romantic relationships.

_____

_____

_____

_____

Ways to Deal with Shoulds

1. Take a second look at your expectations of others. Ask yourself if your expectations are unrealistic.

2. Start thinking in terms of "it would be better if" instead of "they should."

3. Realize that life is not fair and that others don't always—and possibly seldom—share your values. If you are only going to be happy when people behave as they "should," then you are guaranteed to feel angry, hurt, and resentful.

Feeling Like a Victim

At the beginning of this chapter, I defined self-efficacy as a person's ability to have control and enact change in his or her life. You cannot have a sense of power and control in your life if you feel like a victim.

Because of childhood experiences, many adults with ADD can take on the persona of a victim. After all, we all experienced times when we felt hurt, picked on, and misunderstood because of our symptoms. I can remember my own experience in junior high school. I know that seventh and eighth grades were the worst two years of my life.

I went to school when spankings were still a regular part of school life. One of the things you could get a spanking for is if you were late to class three times. The vice principal just did not get that I would have given anything under the sun to be organized enough to get to class. The fact of the matter was that I often had difficulty remembering what class to go to next!

My disorganization and memory problems played out in other ways as well. Well into the year, I would forget my locker combination. I frequently showed up to class without the proper book or proper supplies or without the homework that I had spent several hours struggling through the night before.

The attitude of the time was that if you punished a kid enough, he or she would fall in line. As a result, one year I got four spankings just for being late to class. The spankings, of course, never helped. It only made me feel trapped, frustrated, overwhelmed, and powerless.

I share this story because it is so similar to many of the childhood stories of adults with ADD. Such experiences can clearly make us feel like victims. That being said, carrying around the identity of a victim and/or an oversensitivity to how others treat us unfairly can make for further problems as adults. Due to our victim identity, we feel powerless to enact change in our own lives. We rob ourselves of happiness and contentment.

In his book, *Happiness Is a Serious Problem: A Human Nature Repair Manual*, Dennis Prager (1998) does a marvelous job of showing why it is important to not view yourself as a victim. While this book is not about ADD, the messages in it are universal. Prager points out that there are some clear rules about happiness. One of these rules is that you cannot be happy if your primary identity is that of a victim, even if you really are one. He gives the following reasons why this is the case:

- People who sees themselves as victims do not view themselves as being in control of their lives. Happiness happens *to* them and not because of what they do.

- Those who view themselves as victims see the world as unfair, particularly to them.

- People who regard themselves as victims have a tendency toward anger, and an angry disposition makes happiness impossible.

- If you view yourself as a victim, then it is impossible to enjoy life because enjoying life would challenge your self-perception.

How Feeling Like a Victim Affects Relationships

If you a tend to view yourself as a victim, it is impossible to have a happy and healthy relationship. You will tend to do the following things in your relationships:

Complain about how you are being treated unfairly. This could play out by your coming home and constantly complaining about how you were being treated unfairly at work. It could also be seen in complaining to your spouse or lover about how he or she treats you unfairly.

Filter out positive aspects of the relationship and focus only on what seems to be unfair toward you. A colleague of mine has a plaque in his office that reads, "Sometimes you're the statue. Sometimes you're the bird." Individuals who have a tendency to see life as unfair are very well aware of when they are the statue, but they negate the times when they are the bird. You might become attuned to when things do not work out in your favor in your relationship, but not notice the times when they do.

Have an angry or irritated disposition toward your spouse or lover. Individuals who feel like they are always being treated unfairly have a much greater likelihood of developing an angry disposition toward others, and this makes relationships extremely difficult.

Be a real drag to be around. If your primary identity is that of a victim, then it can be extremely difficult to enjoy your time with your spouse or lover; to enjoy yourself goes against your primary identity.

Filtering

As I have already mentioned, victims are more likely to realize when they are not being treated fairly than when things are going well for them. They filter out, or discredit, those times. In fact, filtering is the most common form of irrational thinking that victims do.

Prager (1998) talks about how expectations can lead to dissatisfaction, but they don't lead to happiness. Just think about it. If you expect others to treat you fairly, you are not especially happy when they do. If, however, they do not treat you fairly, then you get angry, hurt, and upset.

Filtering leads to similar results. If you filter out the positives, you will have a hard time appreciating a roof over your head, food in your stomach, a child who is doing well in school, a job that pays the bills, or a million other blessings. Instead of appreciating the good that life brings, all those opportunities for joy can be demolished because all you notice is that one person in the office who does not work as hard but gets paid more money than you do.

The following exercise helps you identify events that have set you up to feel like a victim. It helps you take personal responsibility for having maintained a victim identity. It helps you count the blessings in your life that challenge that identity. And it identifies what you need to do to take responsibility for change.

Exercise 4.4

What are the things that have happened in your life, including your childhood, that cause you to feel like you were treated unfairly or have been misunderstood? _____

_____

_____

_____

_____

How do you allow these things to rob you of a sense of happiness and to have a negative impact on your relationship? _____

_____

_____

_____

_____

What things do you have to be grateful for? In what ways are you blessed? (List at least twice as many blessings as the number of negatives you've listed.) _____

_____

_____

_____

_____

What things do you need to take responsibility for in your own life to quit feeling like a victim? _____

_____

_____

_____

✳ ✳ ✳ ✳ ✳

This is hard work, but by becoming more aware of your feelings of victimization and your irrational thought patterns, you will learn not to respond to others in the same old ways. You will be able to identify when you are falling into old insecurities that limit you. The old ways of thinking are not just going to go away, but now you can begin to see when you are thinking irrationally, and you will be better able to challenge your irrational thoughts instead of just accepting them as truths. You will not just assume that you will fail. You will not just assume that others are thinking poorly of you. You will not just automatically feel that you do not have control in your own life. This will bring greater freedom in your life and flexibility in your relationships.

Chapter 5

Sensitive Spots

If you have ADD, you have probably experienced a number of difficulties when others have not understood the impact of your ADD. As a child, you might have felt that others considered you lazy or stupid due to your disorganization or difficulty completing tasks, and you might have been punished when you were sincerely struggling to gain control of your condition. As a result, you may have developed sensitive spots; these are emotionally charged areas that are easily triggered.

Coping with Childhood Issues

The following story shows how childhood issues play a role in our lives as adults.

Clarice's Story

In many ways Clarice is one of the most remarkable people I have ever met. Clarice had many things going against her, the least of which was having ADD. When Clarice was younger, her mother had abandoned the family. Clarice's father had been highly uninvolved, and she had experienced abusive relationships and childhood poverty. She was able to finish high school, but did not go to college. In spite of all this she rose to a position in her company that often requires a college education and she put her own children through college.

Even with all her accomplishments, Clarice still had several sensitive spots. She frequently felt that people were talking about her (the irrational belief of "mind reading") because she could remember neighbors and schoolmates making fun of her and her family when she was a child. Because of her ADD, along with her poverty and lack of parental support, school was very difficult for Clarice. Thus, she was very sensitive to the possibility that people did not have faith in her or did not feel that she was competent. As a result, she spent a lot of her time angry. She had learned to build walls around herself to protect herself emotionally.

When Clarice came to understand that many of her reactions were based on childhood sensitivities and not true responses to what was going on between herself and others, she became much more open and relaxed. Not only was she less angry, but she became able to approach life more courageously. She lived near Washington, D.C. and had never trusted herself to drive into the city on her own. During the course of therapy, she started doing this and began going to concerts and other things that she had missed over the years. She got to the point where she would no loger allow her insecurity or her paranoia to get in the way of enjoying life.

As this story illustrates, childhood events may make us more sensitive to certain issues. While you may not have experienced quite the same number of traumatic events as Clarice, you probably have your sensitive spots. For instance, your ADD symptoms, such as having difficulty organizing things, forgetfulness, and difficulty with concentration and focus, might have significantly affected your performance in school. You may have had learning disabilities as a child, and your hyperactive behavior might have made you an easy target for ridicule in school from early on. You might have been the one most likely to be reprimanded by the teacher because your voice was just a little louder. Your parents might have been frustrated by your difficulty getting schoolwork done and might have attributed this to laziness.

Coping As an Adult

Today, these childhood experiences still have an impact. For instance, you might show a strong emotional reaction to a significant other stepping in and taking care of things. You might interpret this as your lover feeling that you are incompetent and can't do things on your own.

I know that this happened with my wife and me. By nature, I am a person who likes to put things off (even though I have worked to change my behavior in this area). My wife, on the other hand, is someone who likes to take care of things as soon as possible. She lives by the motto that "one only plays when the work is done and the work is never done." Because of this she would easily get frustrated with me when things did not get taken care of in her time frame. Instead of realistically seeing that she just needed to have things taken care of before she could unwind and relax, however, I interpreted her frustration as a judgment of me. I felt that she had judged me as incapable of taking care of things on my own.

It was only when I was able to quit making the issue about me that I was able to see her needs and meet them to a much greater degree. As a result, our relationship improved.

Feeling Stupid

One of the most common sensitive spots I have observed in my adult ADD patients relates to "feeling stupid." Because this sensitive spot obviously stems from a multitude of childhood issues for ADD adults, the feeling is easily triggered by many behaviors on the part of a spouse or lover.

The feeling is often triggered when a significant other attempts to be helpful. For instance, if you are having difficulty thinking through the steps to complete a task, the significant other might jump in and do it for you. The reaction to this helpfulness can be, "What, don't you think I can take care of this on my own?" The interpretation is "you think I'm stupid," when the real intent might have been just to be helpful.

Because of sensitive spots, ADD adults can be especially prone to the irrational thought pattern of mind reading. Mind reading involves your making assumptions about the intent or motivation behind the behavior of others without checking out those assumptions. The next story demonstrates how mind reading can create conflict in relationships.

Beth and Paul's Story

Beth and Paul had been married for three years. In spite of his ADD, Paul was a very good salesman. He always had the top number of sales each year and was a real go-getter.

Paul had significant difficulty in school, particularly in math. He could remember several battles with his mom and dad over getting his math homework done. He had difficulty thinking through the steps of a math problem. He remembered how stupid and incompetent he felt as a kid when he struggled with math.

Both Beth and Paul hated tax season. Paul insisted on doing the taxes himself. Beth, however, had a background in accounting and wanted to double-check his work just to make sure they got every deduction they could. She also felt a little resentful that even thought she had the background in accounting he insisted on doing the taxes by himself. Every time she would try to help, and especially when she found something to correct, Paul would become very angry. He would often respond to Beth by screaming, "Don't you think I can do any freaking thing on my own!" Both Paul and Beth would be left feeling hurt. Beth would feel that Paul did not respect her and Paul would feel that Beth thought he was stupid and incompetent.

Exercise 5.1

Consider some of your childhood experiences. What happened in your early school experience that made you feel stupid, incompetent, or isolated and/or rejected by others?

_____

_____

_____

What happened at home that made you feel stupid or incapable? What unintentional messages did your parents send (such as "you're lazy") that have created sensitive spots for you as an adult? _____

_____

_____

_____

How do these sensitive spots affect your relationship? What unfounded assumptions do you make about why your significant other does certain things? In other words, how do you display mind-reading tendencies? _____

_____

_____

_____

What are the specific kinds of circumstances in which your significant other is likely to inadvertently touch on a sensitive spot? _____

_____

_____

_____

After you have identified your sensitive spots and how they contribute to mind reading, you need to develop alternative ways of reacting. This often simply involves checking out your assumptions. Instead of just assuming that you know the motivation behind what your partner is doing or saying, you need to learn to ask him or her about it. By checking out your assumptions, you avoid automatically reacting to them.

If you have read any self-help literature on couples counseling, or have been to a couples therapist, you have probably heard of " 'I' statements." "I" statements help couples communicate about their feelings without casting blame on the other person. This simply means learning to say something like, "I feel that right now you are saying that I can't take care of this on my own."

You can try this technique to discuss some of your sensitive spots. It would be a good idea to set aside some time to sit down with your partner. Let your partner know that this involves your own issues and that you are not judging him or her when you make your "I" statements. You are simply doing your part to try to keep your own personal issues from getting in the way of a healthy relationship. A caring partner will be willing to work with you.

Chapter 6

Avoidance

It is clear that people with ADD often use stimulation as a way to self-medicate. We also will often avoid things that require an extended period of concentration and focus. The problem is that we still need to take care of things that are not stimulating and/or require an extended period of concentration and focus. There is just no way around it, no matter how much we avoid, ignore, scream, or cry. There are things that still have to get done. We can go through the stress and emotional misery of putting these things off, or we can deal with them in a proactive manner.

We are often great at making wonderful arguments for why the more interesting or stimulating tasks have to be taken care of right away and the less interesting tasks can be put off until later. It is often not until the less stimulating tasks become crisis-driven that we take care of them. This can often make us feel as if we are under a great deal of pressure much of the time. The truth is, however, that we do this to ourselves by consistently choosing what we want to do until what we have avoided becomes what we have to do.

Learn to Avoid Avoidance

The reality is that we spend more time on the less interesting things by avoiding them:

1. When we wait until we are in crisis mode to get things done, we make careless mistakes that have to be corrected later.

2. We have to remember things that we would not have had to struggle to remember if we had taken care of them right away.

3. We have to take the time to have a conflict with our spouse or significant other over it when we could have of just taken care of the task in the first place.

4. We have to waste all that time putting emotional energy into avoiding the task.

5. We have to find whatever we need to take care of the task, which could have been avoided if we had taken care of the task right away.

If you don't believe the above things are true, then just think about that paperwork you put off at work. How long does it take you to look up everything you need, find everything you need, and remember everything you need, to get the paperwork done? How rushed do you feel when you are doing it? How much easier would it be and how much time would it save if you did not find excuses to put the paperwork off and, instead, took care of it right away? How much less would you have to worry and how much less grief would you get from your boss and coworkers?

Think also about all the things you avoid putting where they belong right away and all the things you have avoided finishing just because it makes you cringe at the thought of having to do them. For instance, how long have you dug through a messy home office or a messy basement or garage because you can't stand the thought of cleaning it up? It might even get to a point that you avoid going into your home office or garage. If you really put your mind to it, you could probably get that office cleaned up in one weekend. Instead of doing that, you choose to deal with arguments from your spouse and effectively choose to lose some major square footage in your home.

Also, think about how it makes you feel every time you go through that office or garage. Think what it is like every time you need a given piece of paperwork or a given tool and you have to spend an inordinate amount of time looking for it as you shuffle things from pile to pile. How much better would it be to commit to taking care of it and then commit to keeping it organized? That means you commit to putting things away the first time and never saying to yourself, "I will put it away later."

What I am talking about is not just straightening up your home office or garage or taking care of your paperwork. I am asking you to truly embrace the idea that avoidance causes a great deal of unnecessary frustration and grief in your life. You need to clearly understand that the best way to avoid things is not to avoid them. If you would take care of things right away instead of avoiding them, then they would take less time, effort, and emotional energy. Here is a great rule of thumb: Figure out whatever you want to do least and take care of it first. If you put this into practice, you will experience a large reduction in the amount of anxiety, tension, and conflict in your life.

How Avoidance Affects Romantic Relationships

The primary thing that avoidance can do in relationships is make your spouse or lover feel insignificant or unimportant. Whether you intend it to or not, avoiding taking care of things that are important to your significant other can communicate to him or her that "my needs are not important to you." There is obviously no way that a relationship is not harmed when your significant other feels unimportant in your life. This next story of a couple I counseled gives a good example of the impact that avoidance had on a relationship.

Rob and Emily's Story

Emily and her husband, Rob, had made the decision that Emily would stay at home after the birth of their first child. Emily, the spouse with ADD, had been an EMT technician. She had loved her job because it had provided her with a great deal of stimulation. Her new job as stay-at-home mom, however, did not give her the same level of excitement. As a result, she sought out other ways to increase her stimulation at the expense of household chores.

Rob had previously taken on most of the responsibility for household chores when the two of them had both worked outside the home. He repeatedly pointed out that he had not expected Emily to quit her job. He said that he was happy for her to be a stay-at-home mom if that was what she wanted, but that part of the agreement between the two of them was that she would be willing to take over certain chores on a weekly basis. She had agreed to do this initially without reservation. In fact, she had been emphatic about it. She would take care of the chores discussed because she knew how important it was to Rob to have a clean and neat home. Rob, however, soon found himself doing the dusting and the mopping because what had been previously done on a weekly basis was now taking two or three weeks.

Apparently Emily hated housecleaning. She found dusting and mopping and changing diapers excruciatingly boring. She would find excuses to go over to her mother's house or a friend's house most of the time. This left her little time to take care of the things she had agreed to do. Rob was left feeling angry and resentful. Emily, on the other hand, felt that Rob was being controlling.

After a careful examination of the way the chores were being divided up, it became clear that Rob was not being unreasonable. As a matter of fact, even if Emily had done the agreed-upon chores, Rob still would have been doing approximately half the household work, in addition to putting in ten-hour days.

I calculated the amount of time it would have taken Emily to do the chores that she had agreed to do. The total time per week was roughly two hours. I then calculated the amount of time the couple spent arguing over the chores or feeling hurt and resentful toward one another. That averaged out to about seven hours a week. In reality, however, this calculation was rather conservative because Rob had stopped doing some of the nice things for Emily that he had previously done. He had decided, "If she does not care about my needs, I am not going to worry about hers." The reality was that Emily's avoidance of a few chores that took a relatively small amount of her time per week was triggering events that were placing the relationship in jeopardy. How much easier would it have been to just fight through the avoidance and do the two hours' worth of chores?

Confronting the Problem

To get rid of avoidance in your life, you first have to be able to identify what you avoid. Do the following exercise with the help of your partner.

Exercise 6.1

In the space provided, write down the things you regularly avoid. Make a complete list, then answer the questions that follow. _____

_____

_____

_____

How does avoiding these things increase stress for you? _____

_____

_____

_____

What kind of impact does avoidance have on your relationship? _____

_____

_____

_____

What things do you feel you can commit to not avoiding for the sake of yourself and for the sake of your relationship? _____

_____

_____

_____

✳ ✳ ✳ ✳ ✳

In this exercise, you identified what it is that you regularly avoid and you have stated your commitment to stop avoiding at least some of these things. What is your plan to make sure you stick to your commitment? For instance, if you are making a commitment to no longer avoid household chores, you might make an agreement with yourself and your partner to get the chores out of the way the first thing every weekend. Whatever you are avoiding, you need to have a specific plan to deal with the avoidance. It is often good to talk to your romantic partner about your avoidance issues and come up with a plan together.

Of course, it is important that your partner support your efforts. You will need to work out with your partner what will feel supportive for you, as well as what kind of support your partner will be able to give without feeling burdened and resentful.

Chapter 7

ADD, Stimulation, and Romantic Relationships

There are a variety of ways in which an ADD adult's need for stimulation can impact romantic relationships. You should be aware of how stimulation issues play out in your relationship so you can monitor your response to your need for stimulation. The ADD partner's need for stimulation can lead to much fun and excitement for a couple. It can also lead to a great deal of disconnectedness and hurt feelings if not appropriately monitored.

Hyperfocusing

Hyperfocusing is the act of concentrating on something intensely. To truly understand what hyperfocusing is in relation to the ADD condition, you need to recall the neurological cause for ADD. As I pointed out in chapter 2, ADD is not truly an attention problem or a hyperactivity problem. Those are just the by-products of the underlying neurological condition. We are really dealing with a neurological understimulation disorder. In chapter 2, I gave the example of the child with ADD and a video game. That same child who shows extreme difficulty concentrating and focusing in the classroom will be able to sit in front of the video game and play for hours on end. In fact, try to drag him away from the game and you may have a full-blown temper tantrum on your hands.

The fact of the matter is that many adults and children with ADD, particularly those who display hyperactive characteristics, crave stimulation. Because of this, when they find something that does get the neurons firing, they will often overfocus or "hyperfocus" on it. This can have a devastating impact on relationships. If an individual with ADD is spending an inordinate amount of time on the Internet, playing computer games, or doing whatever else fills his or her craving for stimulation, the relationship will undoubtedly suffer. Relationships are like plants. If they are well tended, they will grow. If neglected, they will wither and die.

If you have hobbies or interests that take up a significant amount of time and you are in a relationship, you need to make a special effort to be aware of the needs of your partner. It is vital that time be set aside for the two of you. For instance, let's say that you are a major football fan. You might look forward to the football season all year long. You love going to the games or having buddies over on Sunday. If nothing else, you like sitting in front of the television watching games on weekends and on Monday nights as well.

Let us also say that your partner is nowhere near as big a football fan as you are. Your partner begins to express anger and resentment about the time you spend on this pastime. This leads to several conflicts. You begin to feel that every interaction with your partner is unpleasant. You start finding other reasons to avoid your partner because you don't want to be "nagged." This leads to even greater resentment, and the problem escalates. You do not know what went so wrong. The relationship started off so well and now everything has gone to pot! The person that made you feel so good now seems to make you feel so miserable.

What you have forgotten is that your behavior probably changed first. In fact, you might have met this wonderful person during football season two or three years ago. Because the relationship was exciting and new, you spent very little time focusing on football and a great deal of time on the relationship.

People with ADD are often magnetically attracted to whatever is new and exciting. Because ADD is a neurological condition of understimulation, we are often attracted to things which increase stimulation. New relationships do a great job at this. The problem with new relationships is that they do not stay new forever. There comes a point when watching guys crash into one another on the field of battle becomes more stimulating than some person you see day in and day out. As a result your focus shifts off of your sweetheart and onto football. Over time, this causes your partner to sour toward you.

What to Do about Hyperfocusing Behavior

There are several steps you can take to keep your relationship in strong working order. For instance, you can schedule times to have dates with your partner. In fact, it is good to have a regularly scheduled date night. This is true, no matter if you have children or not. When they have children, many people seem to forget that they need to continue to take time for their marriage. The fact of the matter is that if you are always putting your children first and your marriage second, you are setting yourself up for a poorly maintained marriage. When that happens, everyone, including the children, suffers.

It is also a good idea to limit the time you spend on your hobbies and interests. For instance, you might limit yourself to watching a certain number of football games or to watching football games on only one night per week. You could spend another night doing something with your sweetheart as an expression of love. You will feel a whole lot better doing this because you love your partner than because you do not want him or her to "nag" you. You are doing something positive, instead of avoiding something negative. This approach will also feel much better to your partner.

If you are doing something for your sweetheart, however, make sure you let him or her know in advance. If you want to watch the Redskins and Cowboys game on Monday night, but you are not going to watch any football on Sunday night so that you can spend some time with your partner, then say so ahead of time. This will work a whole lot better than saying on Monday night, "Well I gave you my time all day yesterday, what else do you want!" Plan in advance, and you will save yourself a great deal of trouble.

My final suggestion is to follow the concept of "the love bank," described in chapter 16. This is a very important concept for anyone with or without ADD and will go a long way toward keeping a relationship strong.

The following exercise will help you gain control over your tendency to hyperfocus.

Exercise 7.1

On what things are you most likely to hyperfocus? _____

_____

_____

_____

What is your plan, based on the above recommendations, to deal with your hyperfocusing behavior? What do you specifically plan to do to get a handle on things so that hyperfocusing tendencies do not negatively impact your relationship? _____

_____

_____

_____

_____

✳ ✳ ✳ ✳ ✳

The Missing Tile Syndrome

I was introduced to the idea of the "missing tile syndrome" in Dennis Prager's book *Happiness Is a Serious Problem: A Human Nature Repair Manual* (1998). Prager points out that one of the most effective ways of sabotaging happiness is to look at a beautiful picture and fixate on what is flawed or missing. He asks the reader to imagine looking at a tiled ceiling from which one tile is missing. Usually people concentrate on the missing tile, he says. In fact, he adds, the more beautiful the ceiling, the more likely you are to concentrate on the missing tile and permit it to affect your enjoyment of the rest of the ceiling.

The missing tile syndrome represents our tendency to focus on what is flawed or missing rather than to find beauty or joy in what is there.

In general, people with ADD are not as apt to "notice the missing tile" initially. We can start off loving that new relationship. It is not until after the novelty has warn off that we begin to notice all the missing tiles. We feel that it is those missing tiles that are making us miserable, when in reality it may be that the new relationship is just no longer providing us with the stimulation that we crave. This can lead to our jumping from relationship to relationship. We think it is our current relationship that is making us unhappy when, in reality, it is just the fact that the "newness" is gone.

This tendency to blame our relationship problems on what is missing, instead of looking at the internal issue, can lead to a highly chaotic romantic history if we do not keep it in check. Happiness with a partner does not come from finding the perfect person. There will always be missing tiles in any romantic relationship. If we expect the picture to be perfect, then we will never be fully in our relationships.

The most common missing tile I have seen in the ADD adults with whom I have worked is the "I just don't feel in love" tile. Many adults with ADD experience life in a highly kinesthetic way. We crave stimulation in whatever form that it can be achieved to make ourselves feel more comfortable in our own skin. A new relationship can be highly stimulating. Because of this, ADD adults can become highly engrossed in the new relationship since it feels so good. When the relationship no longer provides the necessary stimulation that we crave, however, we can feel as if "the magic is gone." This can lead to the untimely termination of a perfectly good relationship. The following story is a case in point.

Linda's Story

Linda was a friendly and vivacious forty-seven-year-old. Even though she seemed like a great deal of fun and was someone with whom others appeared to get along easily, she seemed to have a lot of difficulties with long-term relationships. She had been married in her early twenties to a fellow named John.

Linda initially said that she was not sure if she ever loved John. Upon further exploration, however, she described a relationship that started out as highly romantic. She talked about how special John would make her feel. John would bring her flowers and would take her places. He seemed to really love her. She admitted that even until the end he "treated her like a queen." She said that the spark "just was not there."

Linda's relationship with John ended after she was caught having an affair with a man named Larry. She reported that the heat was there with Larry. He was a "tiger in bed" and "rocked her world." She said, however, that the sex was just not enough. Apparently Larry was a great lover but not a great conversationalist. Their relationship lasted about six months and then she terminated it.

Linda never got married again. She did, however, have a long history of relationships that lasted from six months to one and a half years. She reports that she normally would enjoy the relationships for six months to a year, but then would become bored with them. It would be around that time that she would become acutely aware of some flaw, or "missing tile," within her partner that would lead her to become highly dissatisfied. She would then ruminate on that flaw until she could use it as justification for terminating the relationship.

Through counseling, it became apparent that Linda had been involved with several men who would have made good mates. She had just become bored with each relationship after the "newness" wore off. Linda did not have problems with low self-esteem. She was not replaying her relationship with her father. She did not even particularly have a fear of commitment. She had a misunderstanding of what relationships were supposed to provide. She allowed her need for constant stimulation within a relationship, as well as a desire to meet an unrealistic expectation that she would always feel passion, to ruin several good opportunities for a meaningful long-term relationship.

If you related to this story at all, do the following exercise.

Exercise 7.2

Now would be a good time to think back on your past relationships. By considering how the missing tile syndrome has impacted past relationships, you will be reducing the likelihood of it having a negative impact in the future. You will be recognizing it for what it is. Answer the following questions in the spaces provided.

How does the missing tile syndrome apply to your past and current romantic relationships? What excuses do you repeatedly use to end relationships? _____

_____

_____

_____

What do you need to change about the way you view problems in your relationships? What unreasonable expectations do you hold (such as I will always feel that warm, fuzzy feeling) that are leading you to be repeatedly dissatisfied with your relationships? _____

_____

_____

_____

To increase the likelihood of having a successful long-term relationship, what changes do you need to make in your expectations? _____

_____

_____

_____

✱ ✱ ✱ ✱ ✱

By identifying unrealistic expectations you have about relationships, and replacing those unrealistic expectations with realistic ones, you will stand a much better chance of having a good, healthy relationship.

Stimulation and Disconnection

From an early age, many people with ADD can remember feeling a physical sense of discomfort when there was not enough stimulation in their environment. A lot of us learned very early on how to decrease our sense of physical discomfort (that ants in the pants feeling) by seeking immediate gratification from others. We expected others to listen immediately or to let us continue to do whatever activity was stimulating, regardless of what was going on with them. If they did not meet our need, we may have been willing to persist and wear them down until we got our need for stimulation met.

Another way of thinking of this is to think of stimulation as a drug. When we get stimulation, we feel better, so we want it. This need has always been there, and so we learned how to focus our life around meeting the need. What often got lost in the process was the needs of others. Who cares if mom needs to go to the store? I am still playing my video game! Who cares if other people are talking? I have something that I want to say right now!

Because we were so caught up in getting our stimulation fix, we became unaware of how our excitable and demanding behavior affected others. We didn't understand when other kids did not want to play with us or why mom and dad looked upset at us so often and told us to go to our room. We didn't get why we always seemed to be the one that the teacher reprimanded or had to go to the principal's office. After all, we were not trying to be bad. We just wanted to have fun and be liked. In response, we felt misunderstood, isolated, and alone. In short, we were disconnected from the needs of others and, at the same time, we felt misunderstood by others.

Just because our need for stimulation contributed to feelings of disconnection as children, however, does not mean that we have to continue this pattern into adulthood, repeating the same mistakes. As children we did not clearly understand the problems that our craving for stimulation caused for us and others. By adulthood, it is possible that our craving for stimulation has become a negative habit. If this is the case for you, then you must recognize the negative patterns that the need for stimulation has established in your relationships and be willing to change.

You have to be more aware of the needs of others by understanding when you are acting like a stimulation junky at the expense of the needs of others around you. Your romantic partner has reason to be upset if you spend all your time on the computer playing games or always get caught up in your new and exciting project at the expense of his or her needs.

Exercise 7.3

To determine if you suffer from a stimulation addiction, ask yourself the following questions.

- Do I cut my partner off when he or she is speaking because I have a strong urge to express myself?

- Does my partner feel neglected when I get caught up in something new or stimulating?

- Do I find myself expressing anger toward my partner a great deal of the time?

- Do I tend to make promises to my partner and not keep them because I find myself getting caught up in something else I would rather do?

- Do I like to pick at and tease my partner?

- Do I sometimes like arguing with my partner because it is exciting and/or stimulating?

- Do I interrupt my partner when he or she is doing something else, just because I am so bored and I want him or her to entertain me?

- Do I find my partner getting upset at me, yet I persist at whatever is upsetting or annoying him or her because I find it entertaining?

- Do I often wonder why my partner is angry or upset with me so often?

- Do I find myself confused over why my partner makes such a big deal out of things that I do?

✳ ✳ ✳ ✳ ✳

If you answered "yes" to very many of the questions above, you would probably benefit from taking a serious look at your stimulation addiction:

1. Practice becoming aware of how your behavior affects your partner and others.

2. Practice becoming more aware of the needs of your partner and others.

3. Practice relaxation techniques.

4. Learn to refocus your energies in appropriate and productive ways.

5. Learn to communicate more effectively with your partner and others.

6. Consider an evaluation for neurostimulant medication.

Exercise 7.4

To help yourself become a better self-observer and have greater control over your craving for stimulation answer the following questions:

How does your need for stimulation negatively impact your romantic relationships? ____

_____

_____

_____

_____

What changes do you need to make in response to your need for stimulation for it to stop having a negative impact? _____

_____

_____

_____

_____

Once you have made these changes, how would your romantic partner be able to know you have made them? What should he or she be able to observe? _____

_____

_____

_____

_____

✳ ✳ ✳ ✳ ✳

Discuss with your partner the best way to implement these changes. Maybe he or she can let you know when you are acting like a stimulation junkie in a way that does not tap into your sensitive spots.

Confusing Stimulation and Fun with Happiness

Before you read on any further, imagine a group of happy people. What do they look like? Where are they? What are they doing? You might have imagined a group of people whose team is winning at a sporting event or a group of people at a party or a group of people white-water rafting down a river. Did you, however, imagine an old couple sitting on a porch recollecting a lifetime of memories together? Did you imagine a young married couple experiencing the joys of their first child? Did the things that you imagine involve temporary happiness, or did your thoughts focus on things that had true, lasting meaning?

For some adults with ADD, especially the hyperactive/impulsive subtype, stimulation can be seen as a requirement for a happy and fulfilling life. This belief dooms many relationships. Long-term relationships are not made up of one party after another, and they are not self-sustaining. If you intend on having a long-term relationship, then you will have to endure times that are boring. You will have to accept that there will be things that you do not like about your love, yet also accept the whole of who he of she is anyway. This means that you will have the opportunity to look beyond your need for stimulation and excitement. You will have the opportunity to know someone's true self and not just what you find stimulating and exciting.

A loving and accepting relationship can be a powerfully healing experience. With time, every possible healthy and dysfunctional aspect of yourself and your love will be brought to light through your interactions. Relationships provide the ground for nurturing those healthy aspects of ourselves, and healing those damaged aspects of ourselves. As you learn to connect with another human being on a real level, you learn to connect with yourself. What a wonderful and difficult opportunity!

Prager (1998) does a good job of distinguishing the difference between fun (stimulation) and happiness. He points out that whereas fun is temporary, happiness is ongoing. Too many people decide to commit to a relationship because the other person is "fun." The fact that the sex is great, for example, is not enough of a reason to commit to someone.

EXERCISE 7.5

Take a moment to stop and think about what you would need to truly be happy with someone for years to come.

What values would you need to share? What characteristics would that person really need to have to be a good mate? _____

_____

_____

_____

Have you tended in the past to impulsively jump into unhealthy relationships. These relationships might have felt good in the beginning, yet you later learned that they were not good for you. What have you learned from these experiences that will make you wiser in choosing a romantic partner in the future? _____

_____

_____

_____

What things have attracted you to other people in the past that, while they might have helped with the initial attraction, did not lead to long-term happiness with them? What was missing? _____

_____

_____

_____

* * * * *

The purpose of these exercises has been to help you observe repeated patterns in your life so that you are better equipped to not make the same mistakes over and over again. With work, you can establish healthier habits, which will result in a more satisfying relationship with your romantic partner.

Chapter 8

Getting Rid of "Frustrations"

"Frustrations" are those things that you put off doing or whatever else is repeatedly an irritation or annoyance in your life. If you repeatedly misplace your keys, for example, you may find yourself often frustrated.

How Frustrations Affect Relationships

Frustration affects relationships in two different ways. First of all, the ADD adult's reaction to frustration can often make him or her unpleasant to be around. He or she may become panicky, angry, or irritable, or all of these things at once.

Frustration can also turn the non-ADD partner into the caretaker of the ADD partner. Over time, this can cause resentment to build within the non-ADD partner. I have heard many a non-ADD partner say, "Why does he expect me to know where his keys are?" Or, "Why can't she be responsible for herself?"

An ironic impact of frustration on relationships is that the ADD partner can actually come to resent the non-ADD partner for taking care of him or her. In fact, non-ADD partners can get placed in quite a double bind. If they don't help the ADD partner, they might have to deal with someone who is angry, irritated, or panicky. If they do try to help, the ADD partner might view the behavior as controlling or might take it as a form of criticism—that is, you might think that your partner is saying that you can't take care of yourself. Either way, the non-ADD partner loses, as the following story illustrates.

Jerry and Martha's Story

Jerry and Martha had been married for fifteen years. It was obvious that they loved one another deeply, but Martha said that she had finally had it with Jerry's anger. She said that he would scream at her demanding an answer to "where are my work boots?" or "where is my wallet?" and would get upset if she did not know. At the same time, if she asked him to put his work boots by the door so that he would know where they were in the morning, he would tell her not to treat him like a child.

Upon further exploration it became clear that, based on other various symptoms, Jerry had undiagnosed ADD. He did not mean to keep his wife walking on eggshells, but that is what he effectively did. With the proper utilization of some of the interventions discussed below and with a positive response to neurostimulant medication, his irritability greatly decreased.

Dealing with Frustrations

If you truly have ADD, I can guarantee you that you are not going to completely get rid of frustrations in your life. I can also guarantee that if you follow some basic principles and develop some healthy practices, and continue these practices for as long as you walk this planet, that your frustrations can be significantly reduced.

For ADD partners who have a tendency to lose or misplace things. The primary principle you need to learn to follow is "Everything has a place, its place is the same place all the time, and I am responsible for putting it in its place as soon as I am done with it." You will probably say to yourself that you have tried living by a similar idea in the past, and that it just does not work for you because you get sidetracked and you just don't remember to put things back. It's not that you don't want to. You just don't think about it.

The truth is that you probably will continue to get sidetracked and forget to put things where they belong as soon as you're done. But you will be more likely to find what's missing before it becomes a problem. Let's take your set of keys for example. Let's say you have a dog and you're arriving home late. You know your dog can't "hold it" too much longer, so you rush through the door to take the dog out. Because you are in such a rush, you throw your keys next to the microwave instead of hanging them on the hook where they belong. Later, you walk by the hook where your keys belong and notice they are not there. Instead of waiting until the morning, when you are rushed because you have to get to work, you decide to look for your keys now. You will do this even though your favorite show is on and you would really like to go and watch it. You retrace your steps: You think about what you were doing when you came in. Perhaps you start by looking behind the dog cage and under the table next to the cage. They are not there, but you glance over in the direction of the microwave and you spot them. You hang the keys on the hook.

Now let's take a look at what might have happened if you had decided to go ahead and watch your television program instead of looking for your keys. You might start off by saying to yourself, "I'll look for them when the show is off." Then, after the show goes off, you forget all about looking for your keys because you are thinking about going to bed after you take the dog out for her last walk.

The next morning, you get up to get ready for work. You're running just a little behind, but you know that if you speed up just a little you should be okay. You go over to the hook to get your keys, but they are missing. The dog is in front of you, so you scream at the dog to "Get the heck into your cage." You are already beginning to panic. You look in the pants pockets from the pants you were wearing yesterday. You look in the car to see if you left them there. No such luck. By this point you are frantic. You start looking everywhere for them, and ten minutes later you finally find them.

Now you are in a mad rush to get to work. Instead of driving a little bit over the speed limit, you drive a lot over the speed limit. You wind up getting stopped for speeding and you get a ticket. You finally get to work. Then you realize that you were in such a rush because of the car keys that you left the report you needed for today's meeting in your briefcase, which you left at home. You have to drive home to pick it up. You rush back home to get the report and meet the same police officer you met earlier that day. You now get the pleasure of having your insurance premiums go up and of having to go to court for reckless driving. The officer tells you he "ought to haul you in," but he will settle for seeing you in court. You begrudgingly say thanks and drive on to your meeting. You show up ten minutes late. You are ill prepared. You fake it well enough because you have been in spots like this more times than you like to count. In fact, you can't wait to get off work, so you can drink a cold beverage and relax in front of the television.

Before you go home, though, you have to catch up on some things you could not get done because you had to take that extra trip home and back. By the time you get off work, you are in a rush because you need to get home and take the dog out. You rush through the door and fling your keys on the dog cage. You see them go behind the cage, but you say to yourself that you will hang them on the hook as soon as you get back in. After all, the dog has already been waiting too long. While you're outside with the dog, you start thinking about that cool beverage and your favorite show. You can't wait to unwind from your stressful day. You go to the refrigerator, grab the beverage, kick off your shoes, flip on the tube, and forget all about the keys that still rest behind your dog's cage.

How much easier would it be to just take care of your keys when you are thinking about them?

For the ADD partner who has a tendency to put off things that are going to have to be taken care of later: I hate to sound like a commercial, but "Just do it!" How many times do you stare at that project you have not finished, that pile of papers you have not taken care of, that wall that needs painting, that kitchen that needs cleaning, that employee that needs firing, those taxes that need completing. The list goes on. Every time you look at whatever that thing is, it causes you stress. If you know you are going to have to take care of it anyway, no matter how much you would rather enter a medieval torture chamber than deal with it, why not take care of it? If you tend to avoid doing certain things, which causes frustration, do the following exercise.

Exercise 8.1

Write down five to ten frustrations that you can identify in your life: _____

_____

_____

_____

_____

_____

Now list what you are going to do to get rid of each of these frustrations: _____

_____

_____

_____

_____

_____

_____

_____

✴ ✴ ✴ ✴ ✴

Make a commitment to take care of these frustrations as soon as possible. Make a commitment to stop making excuses. If need be, schedule times in your day planner to take care of these frustrations. You can use this exercise whenever new frustrations emerge.

Stop Frustrating Your Love

Many ADD adults have a tendency to do things that are repeatedly an annoyance, or frustration, for their partners. This can be such things as leaving piles of clothing, or other things, around the house, forgetting appointments, failing to take care of things that you promised to do, and a multitude of other things.

Just as your frustrations can make you feel angry, irritated, upset, and anxious, the things you neglect to do can make your partner feel all those same things. Part of being in a good relationship is being aware of the needs of the other, even when those needs are not your own.

I know that I have had to learn this in my own marriage. When my wife and I got together I was a natural slob. She, on the other hand, liked to have everything neat and orderly. I don't know how many conflicts we had early on about me leaving things lying around the house and leaving piles of stuff everywhere.

Because of my ADD, I certainly had a propensity to jump from task to task and leave things half undone all around the house. For her, this made life with me almost unbearable. When I finally realized that she was not trying to be controlling, but that she had a legitimate need to have things neat and orderly, I was able to quit making the issue about me and start taking care of her needs. Even though it was very difficult to do, I learned to put things away and to avoid cluttering the house. As I reduced these frustrations for her, our relationship improved. She learned to be more flexible over time when I learned to be more considerate of her needs.

If my past patterns with my wife sound at all familiar to you, you might want to consider a marriage counselor. Many people think that a marriage and family therapist is only for couples who are having serious problems. The truth of the matter is that seeing a marriage counselor can improve good relationships. A marriage counselor can be an objective, impartial person who helps the two of you communicate better and be more aware of each other's needs. It would be good to find a marriage counselor who works with adults with ADD. The National Attention Deficit Disorders Association (ADDA) has a list of therapists on their Web page (see appendix D).

I often recommend to couples that they take a personality test called the Myers-Briggs Type Indicator (MBTI). The MBTI identifies your psychological type, based on the theories of Carl G. Jung. He observed that human behavior is not random, but it follows identifiable patterns. The MBTI recognizes sixteen different psychological types. By identifying your type and your partner's type, a therapist certified to administer the MBTI will be able to help the two of you understand each other better. This will result in clearer communication, less conflict, and a greater ability to meet each other's needs.

When my wife and I took this personality test, we learned several things that helped to reduce conflict and improve communication between us. The many things we learned include the following: My wife had a true need to have tasks completed and the house in order or she could not relax. I would frequently get angry at her for not being able to "lighten up" by just being willing to let go of things like getting the dishes done. What I found was that if I would just take a few extra minutes to help her get things done she would be able to relax and we could enjoy being together. I did not have to get angry at her for "not lightening up" and she did not get stuck feeling that I did not care about her needs.

Meanwhile, my wife learned that, because I was what the MBTI termed an *extrovert* and she was an *introvert*, our styles of communication were very different. My wife would often get upset at me because I would say "whatever rolled off the frontal lobe" and I would get angry at her for not responding to my questions quickly enough. Through the use of the MBTI, she learned to let me know when she was still thinking about something and that she would let me know her opinion later and I learned to let her know that I was just thinking out loud about things, and when not to take what I was saying too seriously.

If you would like to learn more about the MBTI or would like to consider meeting with a counselor trained in its use, a good resource is the "personality pathways" (see appendix D). This site provides information on what the MBTI is, has links to other resources and provides a list of trained MBTI-counselors and psychologists.

Chapter 9

Better Living through Organization

In chapter 8, I talked about the importance of reducing frustrations. Now I want to focus on your organization problems because they can make up the lion's share of frustrations for yourself and your partner. If organization problems are not dealt with proactively, it can be very difficult to have a healthy adult relationship. As you become more organized, you will find that both your frustrations and your partner's frustrations will decrease.

Freedom in Structure

People with ADD often feel a physical sense of discomfort when we "have" to do something that we do not "feel" like doing. If you have ADD, then you know what I am talking about. To have to go ahead and pick up that shirt or finish that report before you go home, or straighten up or write down things when you do not feel like it, can make you very uncomfortable. That feeling of discomfort is something that you are going to have to fight to make use of most of my suggestions here. These suggestions can't just become new things to "try," they have to become life habits. They have to become things you do even when you do not feel like it. They have to become things you *just do*.

Once you get into the routine of forcing yourself into these new life habits, you will find that they do not restrict your time and freedom, but actually give you more freedom with your time. You will no longer be in a rush because of stress caused by forgetting things, losing things, or waiting to the last minute to get things done. There is a lot more freedom in life when life is not crisis-driven.

How to Be More Organized

My wife is brilliant at organization. She says, "Get an ordered plan of how things should be done and stick to the same plan each time. Only vary from the plan if you have something that is both urgent and important to take care of."

Before starting a chore or project, my wife will take the time to consider what approach makes the most sense. I used to get frustrated by her planning until I finally realized that she got things done faster than I did because she was not "running around like a chicken with its head cut off." She got things done in an efficient and effective manner. After she figures out the best approach to something, she does not have to think about it the next time. All she has to do is follow the steps she has previously taken. It works.

Here are some other suggestions for how to be more organized.

How to Deal with Paperwork

Adults with ADD are notorious for having piles of papers. I often say that loose leaf paper is one of our worst enemies. There are a few simple rules that can greatly reduce paper as a frustration in your life:

1. **Take care of papers immediately.** Paperwork is often one of the easiest things to avoid. It is also one of the biggest frustrations you will have to deal with if you do not take care of it immediately.

2. **Never touch a piece of paper more than once.** As you are taking care of your paperwork, do not say to yourself, "I will take care of that later." Go ahead and take care of it right away. I can guarantee you that you are just putting off something that you are going to have to take care of later anyhow. Save yourself a lot of unnecessary stress and go ahead and take care of it. Remember that the best way to avoid something is not to avoid it (see chapter 6).

3. **Do one of three things: act on it, file it, or throw it out.** Never put it in a file to take care of later.

4. **Read your mail as soon as you get it and place all mail into one of four categories: pay, answer, file, throw away.** Once again, avoid saying to yourself that you will get to it later. Go ahead and take care of it.

5. **When you pay a bill, immediately date the bill and mark it PAID. Write down the check number and the date.** This is a great memory aid. It will keep you from having to question what you have, and have not, taken care of.

6. **Have one spot in your home where you keep all the bills that need to be paid.** Finding a bill that needs to be paid can be like looking for your keys. You have got to have it but you don't know what you did with it. Before you know it, you are looking everywhere and feeling in a panic. Just like your keys, have one set spot for your bills.

7. **Pay your bills twice a month and put prompts in your day planner to remind you.**

8. **Make an immediate note of anything that needs to be deducted from your taxes and place that note in a specific tax file.**

Create Task Centers

Set up a centralized station that has all the tools and supplies you need to complete a task that you regularly do. For instance, if you use the same cleaning supplies from week to week, then keep all of them in a bucket. That way you can just grab the bucket and go. Have all your laundry supplies in one location. Keep your envelopes and stamps together, along with your address book and a pen. That way you will not have to go looking for a stamp or a pen the next time you want to write a letter.

Create a Family Message Center

Set up a family message center that everyone can check when they get home. An erasable board works well. This message center will help you keep track of where everyone is or whether you need to take care of something.

Create Shortcuts for Yourself

One of my favorite shortcuts is putting spare trash bags at the bottom of the trash can. That way I change the trash bag immediately and will be less likely to forget to put in a fresh bag when I take out the trash.

EXERCISE 9.1

What other shortcuts can you think of for yourself? Write them below:

_____

_____

_____

_____

_____

* * * * *

How to Handle Your Time When You Are Bored

When you are bored at home you can be in danger of neglecting duties and neglecting important relationships by responding to the boredom instead of the needs of others.

For instance, you might play on the computer or in the wood shop when you are bored instead of spending needed time with your significant other or children. You also might start new projects instead of completing old projects, getting the house chores done, or paying the bills.

EXERCISE 9.2

Use the space below to write down ways in which your responses to boredom get you into trouble at home:

_____

_____

_____

_____

There are things that you must do all the time. This list should often include things like daily love investments (see chapter 16), chores, etc. What things do you need to make sure are on your list of essential duties? Use the space below to make a list.

_____

_____

_____

Instead of doing things that are truly not productive, like playing video games or arguing with your significant other, what would be on your list of productive things that you could do to respond to boredom? My list includes things like physical exercise and writing an e-mail to someone that I have not talked to in a long time. Use the space below to make your own list.

_____

_____

_____

* * * * *

How to Use Prompts

One of the defining characteristics of ADD is a difficulty remembering things. Some of the most common kind of memory prompts include day planners, checklists, and sticky notes.

Probably most of you who are reading this workbook have attempted to use prompts, especially visual prompts, at some point in time to assist you in remembering things. If you did not approach the use of prompts with the right frame of mind, your efforts were probably not as successful as you would have liked. There are certain rules that need to be followed when using prompts:

1. Accept that you may have CRS ("Can't Remember Stuff") and that you should have a prompt for anything you need to remember.

2. Set up a prompt immediately for anything that you can't take care of right away. That means if you need to call someone tomorrow, put it in your checklist immediately. If you need to remember to take something to work with you tomorrow, immediately go and find that item so that you can set it by the front door, thus decreasing the likelihood of forgetting it. If you just deposited a check into your account and you need to remember to put it in your checkbook register that is sitting on your nightstand, call your answering machine immediately and remind yourself to put $315.05 in your check register. (If you are using prompts because you are having trouble remembering to do things, but you are expecting yourself to remember to set up the prompts later, then what is the likelihood that your use of prompts will be successful?)

3. When you see the prompt, take care of the task in question ASAP. For instance, when you go home and check your messages, immediately get out your check register and write in a $315.05 deposit. Don't decide to do something else and say to yourself, "I'll get to it later."

4. Make sure your prompts are easily seen. A checklist on a computer in which you have to use a scroll button to see more than three items at a time is not as likely to be as helpful as a checklist in which you can see fifteen items at once. If you can see several items at one glance, then in that one glance you can see all the items you have not taken care of while you are writing the current item down.

5. Keep your prompts organized and simple. Your day planner and checklist should be in some kind of binder together so that you do not have to keep track of more than one item. Don't try to make a complicated system in which you prioritize things. It is best to stick with a simple checklist and a day planner.

6. Don't get overly creative with your prompts. Individuals with ADD often like to change things when they get bored with them. Your visual prompts are not for entertainment purposes. They are tools to help you deal with your CRS.

Kinds of Prompts

The following is a list of various prompts you might find helpful:

- leaving messages on your home-answering machine (to remind you of things you need to remember when you get home)

- leaving messages on your work answering machine (to remind you of things you need to remember when you get to work)

- putting a sticker on your windshield (to remind you when to change your oil)

- setting alarms (to remind you when something is done or it is time to take care of something)

- asking others to remind you (use other prompts as well with this one when possible so that you do not overly depend on someone else for your memory)

- setting out things (so you will remember to take them with you when you leave)

- putting something in your car (so you will remember to take it with you later)

- sending yourself e-mails

- setting up permanent reminders in certain places (if you frequently forget your lunch then take a sticky note and tape the word "lunch" onto your steering wheel)

- using financial and time management computer programs (I personally like the low-tech approach for various reasons, but if you are highly computer literate and would like to utilize the various computer programs that are available then go for it)

No matter how many prompts you use, none of them will work 100 percent of the time. When your prompts do not work, it is good to have a backup plan. You should keep a cellular phone or a pager on your person. That way, if you forget something important, your partner (or child or secretary) can get in touch with you. If you forget to pick up the kids from school, for example, your partner will be able to call and remind you.

Though it's important to take responsibility for yourself with the use of prompts, a backup plan benefits everyone.

EXERCISE 9.3

What other prompts can you think of which would be useful to you? Place your ideas below.

_____

_____

_____

_____

_____

* * * * *

To-Do Lists and Sticky Notes

We have all probably attempted to use to-do lists at some time. They might have been helpful. They might not. The extent to which they are beneficial depends on how you use them. The effectiveness of a to-do list can be maximized if you follow some guiding principles.

Keep one notebook for your to-do list. Do not have several to-do lists. Instead keep one notebook in which you write your items. This notebook should be one that is easy to carry around with you yet will not break your heart if you lose it.

Do not use your to-do list notebook for anything else. Do not write notes from meetings in your to-do list notebook and don't use it for scrap paper or doodling. Simply use it for one-line notes of things you need to remember to do.

When you need to be able to remember something that you cannot take care of right away, then add it to your to-do list immediately. If you wait to write it down, then you will probably forget to write it down. If you have CRS, then accept that you have CRS and don't rely on your memory. Write it down *immediately*.

As soon as you complete an item on your to-do list, cross it out. As you cross out items, you will be able to clearly see the other tasks that you still need to complete.

When you see a task on your list, try to take care of it immediately, if you can. It's always better to complete tasks sooner rather than later. That way, tasks don't pile up.

Always have your to-do list handy. If it is not handy, then how are you going to be able to write things down immediately?

Your to-do list will be your primary memory aid if you use it correctly. It can greatly help you in your day-to-day functioning. Sticky notes can also be useful, to help you remember things in the short term. For instance, if you need to remember to check your dinner in a half hour and you are going in to catch the last few minutes of your TV show, then a sticky note on the remote or TV can be a great prompt.

As a psychotherapist, I always try to remember to transfer my telephone over to the answering service when I start a session. If I cannot do this because I am waiting for a phone call, then I put a sticky note on the phone receiver to remind myself to transfer the phone as soon as my call comes in. Sticky notes are great for things that you need to remember to do before it is time to check your to-do list again.

Shopping Lists

When you are running low on something, like ketchup or soap, it is a good idea to write it down on a shopping list *immediately* so that you will not have to remember it later. This will save you the frustration of running out of things. It will also make shopping more efficient. If I were you, I would post my shopping list in a convenient place, like the refrigerator door.

Day Planners

In addition to helping you remember appointments, day planners can be absolutely invaluable in helping you to remember to be thoughtful. Day planners can help a romantic relationship in the following ways:

1. If you use your day planner appropriately by writing down all your appointments immediately, your love will be a lot less stressed; he or she will worry less about whether or not you are going to take care of things.

2. You will be a lot less stressed because you will not be forgetting important appointments with any kind of frequency.

3. You can put prompts in your day planner reminding you not to forget important dates, such as an anniversary or your love's birthday. You can even put prompts in your day planner to remind you to make plans for your anniversary or to purchase a gift.

4. You can put random prompts in your day planner throughout the year reminding you to "spontaneously" do something thoughtful for your love. This will help remind you to put some focus into your relationship even when you might be hyperfocusing on other things.

Things That Always Need to Be Remembered

There are certain things, such as car maintenance and paying your bills, that always need to be remembered. The following section offers some useful strategies to help you remember to do these things. You can also apply these strategies to various other things that you need to address periodically.

Car Maintenance

I know that it took a couple of serious mechanical problems before I realized that it was important to do the basic maintenance on my car. The fact of the matter is that many adults without ADD have difficulty remembering to maintain their cars. This means that it can be exceptionally difficult for adults with ADD if they do not use some sort of strategy to help them remember. After all, your car is normally not nagging at you to take care of it. It will, however, break down and cost you a great deal of money if you do not take care of it as you should.

Not taking proper care of your car can be dangerous. After all, if you have ignored that squeaking little sound that your break pads make when they are worn out, your breaks might eventually fail. If you don't keep your tires in good shape, you could have a blow out or spin out of control on wet pavement.

Exercise 9.4

Before you get started on this section you need to:

1. Know the average amount of miles your car is driven each week.

2. Have your car owner's manual handy.

3. Have an hour of time to complete the project.

Car manuals typically break down a maintenance schedule by mileage and time intervals. You need to keep this maintenance schedule in your calendar to remember what you need to do to keep your car in good working order. If you are going to use mileage as your indicator, then you need to know the average miles your car is driven on a weekly basis. For instance, if you drive an average of 300 miles a week and you change your oil every 3,000 miles then you would put a visual prompt in your calendar every nine to ten weeks to remind you to change your oil.

Step one: Go through your car manual and figure out all the required maintenance, if any, that has not been completed on your vehicle up to this point. Write down all those items on your to-do list and schedule a time to take care of them.

Step two: Go through the car manual and figure out the required maintenance that will need to be done in the next year. Approximate when the work will be needed and put a reminder in your calendar. Make sure not to forget to put regular reminders for oil changes.

Step three: Don't forget to set up an appointment to take care of the car maintenance as each reminder arises.

✳ ✳ ✳ ✳ ✳

Paying Bills

Forgetting to pay your bills or paying them late will cause you a great deal of headaches. If you are married or living with someone, getting behind on your bills will cause a great deal of stress for your relationship. Staying on top of your bills is a good way to reduce a lot of tension in your relationship.

Exercise 9.5

Step one: Below is a list of the common bills that people pay each month (or each six months, etc.), along with spaces for extra bills that might not be included on this list. Write down the time of the month that each of your bills is due in the section provided.

Bills	Date Due
Cable	
Phone	
Electric	
Gas	
Credit cards	
Cellular phone	
Mortgage/Rent	
Car	
Health insurance	
Car insurance	
Life insurance	

Step two: For each bill, write down a reminder in your calendar seven days before it is due. Put a second reminder five days before it due.

Step three: Pay each bill and stick it in the mail as soon as you see the first reminder. If you don't pay the bill then, make no excuses when you see the second prompt.

By utilizing the recommendations in this chapter, you will feel calmer and more in control. Your life is not going to be as driven by chaos. Over time, if you continue to use these strategies, you will eventually get to the point where you are no longer asking yourself what you have left undone. You will be better able to feel like you are running your life instead of it running you. You will appear more thoughtful and conscientious to your romantic partner and to others in your life. You will just feel better.

Chapter 10

Sharing Responsibilities

For most couples to be happy and avoid resentment, both partners need to feel like the other actively contributes to and shares in the practical day-to-day responsibilities of the relationship. In my work with couples where there is an ADD spouse, I often find distribution of responsibilities is an issue. Various ADD tendencies, such as difficulty staying focused, hyperfocusing, or escaping into pleasurable activities, may get in the way of you doing your fair share.

In her book *Adventures in Fast Forward*, Dr. Kathleen Nadeau (1996) offers some good suggestions for both the ADD partner and the non-ADD partner when it comes to sharing responsibilities. Her suggestions for the ADD partner include:

- Take a look at overcommitments at work that might be robbing you of the energy necessary to participate in commitments at home.

- Use some of your creative energy to notice things that need attention around the home so that you can remove some of the burden from your partner.

- If you tend to gravitate toward "great escapes," like the TV or computer, or your workshop out back, take charge of these patterns.

Exercise 10.1

Take some time now to consider Nadeau's suggestions. Then answer the questions below, writing down your responses.

What types of things are you likely to overcommit to at work to the detriment of your relationship, and what changes do you need to make to give your relationship the attention it deserves? _____

_____

_____

_____

_____

How can you use some of your creative energy to notice things that need attention around the home? _____

_____

_____

_____

What "escapes" get in the way of your responsibilities? What things, such as doing chores and spending time with your love, do you need to attend to before your retreat to your escapes? _____

_____

_____

_____

_____

✳ ✳ ✳ ✳ ✳

Nadeau (1996) also has some suggestions for your partner.

- The non-ADD partner needs to acknowledge different priorities and standards and be willing to compromise. If a high degree of order is important to one of you but not the other, the person who requires the higher degree of order will need to be willing to devote more time and energy to neatness. That does not mean, however, that if you do not require a neat and orderly household, you ignore your partner's need. A successful relationship involves both partners being aware of each other's needs, and learning how to compromise.

- The non-ADD partner might need to take a look at his or her own perfectionism. He or she might be locked in the role of overfunctioning. In response to your ADD symptoms, your partner might have become overfocused on order, responsibility, and things that "must" be done. It is not uncommon for partners to become polarized in relationships. I see this a great deal with couples who have children together. One parent might be highly lenient and the other might be overly strict. (Interestingly, after the breakups between couples where one partner has ADD, the ADD partner often shows a greater willingness to take responsibility for him- or herself.)

The two of you may want to develop separate domains, Nadeau points out. If the ADD partner and non-ADD partner have widely different standards of order, then it is a good idea to carve out separate territories within the home. I have two friends that actually designed their home around this concept. Their home was three stories. While neither one of them had ADD, Ron was a slob whereas Maxine craved neatness and order. Ron kept a playroom in the basement. Maxine, on the other hand, had her sewing room on the third floor. This arrangement provided them both refuges and it also reduced conflict. If Ron started leaving junk around the house, Maxine would just pick it up and toss it in Ron's playroom and Ron was perfectly okay with that. He would just put it away when he felt like it, and he knew to always keep the door to the playroom closed.

You may also want to hire someone else to do tasks that are difficult for you to do and that overburden your partner. Just be practical about it; if hiring a maid helps to reduce a great deal of the conflict and resentments in your relationship, it would be well worth the investment.

Dividing Up Tasks

Nadeau suggests that you take the following into consideration when you divide tasks.

- Given the schedule of each of you, who has the time to do what tasks?

- Who prefers what tasks?

- Which one of you is best suited for a given task?

- Is there anything that you should eliminate by hiring someone else to do it or by changing your lifestyle?

Exercise 10.2

With the above suggestions in mind, I want you to work on the next two tables. In both, the first column contains a list of chores. Place your name in the blanks at the top of column two and your love's name in the blanks at the top of column three.

In the first chart, I want you to look at how chores are currently divided between the two of you. Examine the list with your partner and, for the chores that apply to your relationship, reach some kind of consensus on who does what percentage of each task. I've left extra space for you to add chores (such as childcare activities) not already on the list.

After you have completed the first chart, look at the second chart. This chart is the same as the first chart, except that I want you to use it to redistribute your chores to arrive at a fair division of labor. With the tips at the top of this page in mind, decide between the two of you what would be a fair and reasonable division of labor.

Current Divison of Chores

Chore	Percent of chore for which I, _____, am now responsible.	Percent of chore for which my love, _____, is now responsible
1. Meal planning		
2. Food purchasing		
3. Meal preparation		
4. Kitchen cleaning		
5. Collecting laundry		
6. Washing laundry		
7. Folding laundry		
8. Ironing		
9. Putting laundry away		
10. Depositing and picking up dry cleaning		
11. Straightening up home		
12. Sorting mail		
13. Watering plants		
14. Dumping trash		
15. Vacuuming		
16. Dusting		
17. Cleaning floors		
18. Cleaning bathrooms		
19. Feeding and walking pet		
20. Lawn care		
21. Household maintenance		
22. Financial tasks		
23. Automobile maintenance and repairs		

Fair and Reasonable Division of Chores

Chore	Percent of chore for which I, _____ , am now responsible.	Percent of chore for which my love, _____ , is now responsible
1. Meal planning		
2. Food purchasing		
3. Meal preparation		
4. Kitchen cleaning		
5. Collecting laundry		
6. Washing laundry		
7. Folding laundry		
8. Ironing		
9. Putting laundry away		
10. Depositing and picking up dry cleaning		
11. Straightening up home		
12. Sorting mail		
13. Watering plants		

14. Dumping trash		
15. Vacuuming		
16. Dusting		
17. Cleaning floors		
18. Cleaning bathrooms		
19. Feeding and walking pet		
20. Lawn care		
21. Household maintenance		
22. Financial tasks		
23. Automobile maintenance and repairs		

* * * * *

The purpose of this chapter was not to make sure that everything is perfectly equal between you and your partner in every way. Every couple needs to find out what works best for them. For instance, one of you might like to take care of the bills. I have actually met people who enjoy cleaning the house.

The point of this chapter is to help both of you meet your needs, work as a team, and avoid resentments and power struggles. If your partner and you have accomplished any of these things by going through this chapter, then it was a successful exercise. If you just argued over who does what, then it might be a good idea to see a couples therapist to help resolve the division of responsibilities between the two of you. It is better that you take care of this now than have hard feelings and resentment build over time.

Chapter 11

Learning How to Relax

Stress has many symptoms that can look a lot like ADD. The symptoms that ADD and stress often share include the following:

- anxiety

- overexcitability

- worrying a lot

- becoming easily discouraged

- irritability

- having a bad temper

- frustration

- self-criticism

- confusion

- self-disparagement

- difficultly concentrating

- mind in a whirl

- forgetfulness

How Stress Can Impact Your Relationship

If you already experience many of the above symptoms because of your ADD, then stress does more than just add to these symptoms. Stress has a multiplicative effect. You can become *much* more confused, irritated, angry, discouraged, forgetful, and overwhelmed. Because of this it is important for both your mental health and the health of your relationship that you reduce stress in your life wherever possible. After all, it is no fun to be with someone who is chronically confused, irritated, angry, discouraged, forgetful, and overwhelmed.

Ten Things to Do to Reduce Stress

1. Avoid avoidance (see chapter 6).

2. Reduce frustrations (see chapter 8).

3. Get control of your finances (see chapter 15).

4. If you can do it without putting too much of a financial strain on yourself, hire someone to do some of the things that repeatedly stress you out.

5. If possible, move closer to work to reduce commute time or get another job that is closer to your home so you do not have to deal with traffic as much.

6. Consider simplifying your life. Is having the best of everything really worth it if you are too stressed out to enjoy it?

7. Take action on the things you can change and quit worrying about the things you can't change. This does not mean that you do not care. It just means that you accept that you can't change these things.

8. Learn to meditate so that you can train yourself to physically relax.

9. Take care of yourself physically by getting plenty of sleep and eating properly.

10. Learn to recognize toxic relationships and disengage from them, to the extent that it's possible.

Exercise 11.1

What do you think are the primary ways that you can reduce stress in your life? Be specific in your responses. For example, don't just say, "I'll get more sleep." Instead, write down the time you plan to get in bed each night, no matter what you are hyperfocusing on.

_____

_____

_____

_____

When will you start making each of these changes? Be specific. _____

_____

_____

What are the roadblocks to change? If you can't change certain things, or are unwilling to change them, then how can you reduce the impact that these stressors have in your life (if you can't come up with an answer, then it might be a good idea to discuss these issues with a therapist). _____

_____

_____

✳ ✳ ✳ ✳ ✳

The Fight-or-Flight Response

Besides reducing stress in your life, you can work on improving your response to stress.

You probably have heard of the fight-or-flight response. It is a basic survival response humans share with other animals that tells us to run or fight when we sense danger.

Our bodies respond (to real or imagined threats) with increased heart and breath rate, increased blood pressure, changes of blood flow to the muscles, and so on. In other words, our bodies temporarily go into overdrive to help meet the challenge of a threat or danger. Many of us with ADD, however, can feel like we are in a perpetually stressed state. As a result, our fight-or-flight response might be activated much too much of the time. This can lead to multiple negative consequences for us including

- anxiety and depression

- reduced immunity to disease

- anger and irritability

- diarrhea and/or constipation

- sleep disturbance

- fatigue

- poor concentration

- headaches

- shortness of breath

- weight loss or gain

- increased muscle tension

There are different ways to help reduce the fight-or-flight response. One of the primary ways is to develop a greater sense of mastery and control in your life. This is a long-term commitment. You can also learn to consciously make yourself relax when stressful moments arise. You can do this through meditation and breathing practices.

The Relaxation Response

The relaxation response (RR) was first described by Herbert Benson and colleagues at Harvard Medical School in the 1970s (Benson 1975). Where the fight-or-flight response is like the body's alarm system getting the body ready for immediate action, the relaxation response appears to quiet the body's response to stress. The relaxation response, however, is not automatic. To bring about the relaxation response, you need to practice certain mental techniques. Once you have mastered these techniques, you can use them to counteract stress.

Benson reviewed many religious and philosophical writings. Through this research he realized that there were two primary components to bringing about the relaxation response. These two primary components involved focusing your mind on a repetitive phrase, word, breath, or action and adopting a passive attitude toward thoughts that go through your head.

In *Managing Pain Before It Manages You*, Margaret Caudill (1995) points out that people who regularly practice the relaxation response are less affected by chronic stress. The use of the relaxation response not only has an immediate calming effect, but after about a month of steady practice, people who use the relaxation response on a regular basis show less reactivity to stress in general.

Through my work with individuals who have panic attacks, I have seen how diaphragmatic breathing can reduce the triggering of the fight-or-flight response. Short shallow breaths are characteristic of the fight-or-flight response, and by utilizing diaphragmatic breathing you can inhibit this response.

Shallow chest breathing results in a buildup of oxygen within your blood. If you breathe in a shallow way, you actually build up oxygen with each breath because you are pulling more air in than you are pushing out. The heavier gases, such as oxygen, build up, and the lighter gases get pushed out. This buildup of oxygen within the blood triggers the brain that there is danger. This in turn triggers a whole cascade of physiological responses so that you feel tense, anxious, and possibly in a complete panic.

Just think about it. If someone is hyperventilating, one trick is to have them put a paper bag over their mouth and breathe in and out. This lowers the level of oxygen within the blood. Once the oxygen levels drop below a certain point, the body is fooled into calming itself down.

Caudill (1995) points out that many people breathe from their chests—they expand their chest with each breath instead of their abdomens—because of chronic anxiety, stress, and tension. Because of this chronic tension, along with a focus on having a flat stomach as part of proper posture, our body is essentially conditioned to breathe incorrectly.

As babies, we start off breathing diaphragmatically (breathing in a manner in which our abdomens rise and fall). We only learn to breathe from our chest in response to the impact of prolonged anxiety and social norms regarding posture. Ideally, we should retrain the way we breathe so that we breathe diaphragmatically all the time, and not just during meditation. Diaphragmatic breathing needs to become second nature.

The Relaxation Response and Your Relationship

If you are generally more calm and relaxed, then it is obvious that you will be able to deal with your love in a calmer, more relaxed manner. This can help improve your relationship with your love in the following ways:

1. Your love will not feel like he or she is "walking on eggshells" due to your chronic tension.

2. You will be less likely to say things, or do things, that will trigger anger and hurt in your love.

3. You will be able to learn to identify when you are feeling physically stressed more readily. As a result of this, you will be able to stop yourself before you start spinning out of control or shutting down. This will help to reduce stress and resentment in your love.

4. You will be able to remain in a calm enough state so that you will be able to utilize many of the other recommendations in this workbook instead of just responding to stressors in an automatic manner. Learning the relaxation response will help you learn to observe your physiological responses to stressors. This will help you keep from automatically reacting and, instead, respond to stressors in a calm and relaxed manner.

I had a personal experience that illustrates the point. Around six weeks after I started a meditation practice, something happened that would have normally caused me to spin completely out of control.

My wife is in dental school, and we live about an hour and forty-five minutes away from where she attends school. To help her reduce her drive time, she stays with her sister certain nights of the week. Every Monday I stay at her sister's with her and, as a result, I have to drive an hour to work on Tuesday mornings.

One of these mornings, my wife accidentally set the alarm clock for 4:45 P.M. instead of 4:45 A.M. Luckily, I happened to wake up at 6:00 A.M. My first patient was at 7:00 A.M. That meant that I only had time to drive to my appointment. I did not have time to shower, shave, brush my teeth, or do anything else, for that matter.

My normal reaction would have been to get irritated at my wife (even though I should have been responsible for setting the alarm myself) and then proceed to run around like a chicken with its head cut off. My wife would then have felt nervous and would have frantically worked to help me leave as quickly as possible.

Because of my meditation practice, however, I was able to observe myself going into a fight-or-flight response. I was then able to be a calming force for my wife instead of her being a calming force for me. I told her that no matter what I did I would not be able to do all that I normally did and get to my appointment on time. Since I had seen the couple for a while, they would understand if I was a bit messy in my appearance. Because our home was only five minutes from work, and I did not have an 8:00 A.M. appointment, I would be able to go home for an hour after my first appointment to take a bath and get dressed for the rest of the day.

As you can imagine, my wife was floored. In the past my reactions had been so predictable that she was sure that I would "freak out." She could hardly believe that I was able to handle the situation in such a calm and relaxed manner. She was able to go back to sleep without worrying. Neither one of us felt guilty, angry, hurt, or resentful.

Breathing Exercises

First you need to figure out how you currently breathe. Make sure you are in some comfortable, loose-fitting clothing. Go to your bedroom, or some other quiet place, where you can be relaxed. Lie down on your back. Place one hand on your breastbone and one hand on your belly button. Now take slow breaths in and out. Which hand rises? If it is the hand on your belly button, then you are breathing diaphragmatically. If it is the hand on your breastbone, then you are breathing from your chest.

The exercises below were largely adapted from *Managing Pain Before It Manages You* (Caudill 1995). I've made some changes in wording to make this more applicable to people with ADD. I have used these exercises with several individuals with ADD, anxiety disorders, and anger management issues. I have found them to be very helpful in treating these issues.

Exercise One

1. Find a comfortable place and lie on your stomach.

2. Lift your chest off the floor by bringing your elbows back against your side at the level of your shoulders. Then push off the floor with your forearms (like the Sphinx). This position will arch your back slightly.

3. Breathe normally. This will lock your chest so that when you breathe the abdomen alone will move up and down.

Exercise Two

1. Sit in a chair and clasp your hands behind your head.

2. Point your elbows out to your side. This serves to lock your chest so that you can feel the movement in your abdomen.

3. Breathe normally.

Exercise Three

1. Find a comfortable place and lie on your back.

2. Place your hands just below your belly button.

3. Close your eyes and imagine a balloon inside your abdomen.

4. Each time you breathe in, imagine the balloon filling with air.

5. Each time you breathe out, imagine a balloon collapsing.

Exercise Four

1. Make a tight fist and notice what happens to your breathing. What happens? You probably found that you held your breath or breathed in a shallow manner.

2. Relax your fist.

3. Now, while utilizing diaphragmatic breathing, make a tight fist again. What do you notice about the tension in your fist? It should have been reduced unless you made a truly concentrated effort to maintain the tension. It is actually hard to maintain anger or anxiety and to continue taking deep, diaphragmatic breaths.

Exercise Five

Observe how often you hold your breath when you are feeling overwhelmed or particularly angry or frustrated. You can use diaphragmatic breathing to approach such situations in a calmer manner. When you experience anger or feel particularly anxious or overwhelmed, do the following:

1. Consciously stop and take a pause.

2. Take slow, deep breaths from your diaphragm.

3. Ask yourself, "What am I doing and feeling right now? What is the problem? What choices do I have? How could I handle this situation without getting upset or causing even bigger problems for myself or others?"

As you gain greater control of your body through your breathing, you will feel more in control of yourself and your life. This valuable technique can help you approach life in a calmer manner and be less reactive. Instead of just responding to your fight-or-flight response, you will be the rational human you were meant to be.

As a final tip, I would suggest that you be open to the idea of using meditation techniques and relaxation tapes to help you practice focusing your mind and develop a passive attitude toward thoughts that go through your head. This will help you gain greater mastery of your mind and body. In short, such techniques will help you develop your relaxation response. Besides, it is very useful for someone with ADD to learn to just sit back and relax.

Chapter 12

Dealing with Sarcasm and Anger

Chronic, frequent hostility and sarcasm erode and degrade relationships over time. Interestingly, I have found that in many cases, sarcasm can actually have the greater effect. Sarcasm may be more insidious than outward hostility because it can be masked as humor, and sarcasm can easily become a habit. A sarcastic person may very well deny what is going on, responding to confrontation with something like, "Why are you taking things so seriously? Can't you take a joke?"

Sarcasm

Not all, but many adults with ADD can have a problem with sarcasm. As Fowler and Fowler (1995) point out, sarcasm can almost be expected from an ADD adult. We let our feelings come to the surface easily and we often have an irreverent sense of humor due to our tendency to not think before we speak. The combination of these two things (i.e., the tendency to show our emotions easily and a lack of filtering of the things we say) can often lead to sarcasm.

Sarcasm is clearly damaging to relationships. "It belittles the person being scolded. It gouges at that person's sense of self-worth. It creates fun by causing pain" (Fowler and Fowler 1995, 19). In this context, sarcasm in ADD adults is an expression of control and insecurity, and it is a major issue in the lives of many ADD adults. Since we often feel out of control in many area in our lives, we can use sarcasm as a way of regaining a sense of control. It is a way to regain control by making others feel small.

The following story illustrates the point.

Jim and Frieda's Story

Jim had many of the hyperactive and impulsive characteristics of ADD. In fact, as a child he had been diagnosed with ADD. Neurostimulant medications, however, were not useful for him.

Jim had finished college and was a successful car salesman. He was a real go-getter. Most people felt like he had a great sense of humor and he could make people laugh. Unfortunately, he had gotten into the habit of making Frieda, his fiancé, the brunt of a lot of his jokes. She was able to laugh it off for a while, but over time his jokes wore thin. Even with therapy Jim was unwilling to admit the impact that his sarcasm was having on their relationship. In the end, the wedding was called off. I can tell you that it would not have been called off if Jim had just learned to find another way to direct his humor.

How to Deal with Sarcasm

It is the responsibility of the ADD partner to realize when he or she is being sarcastic. You cannot just blow it off with comments like, "I was just joking. Why do you have to take everything so seriously?"

It is the responsibility of your partner to not let the snide comments go unchallenged. You should encourage your partner to call you on your sarcasm. After all, if you do care about your partner and your relationship, which you likely do if you are reading this book, you would not want to say and do things that are hurtful to your partner.

It is also important that your partner be able to forgive you. Sarcasm is partially a product of ADD. Yes, you are responsible for your behavior, but your partner can help by clearly pointing out the problem. Nothing is gained in a relationship by holding on to resentment.

Exercise 12.1

With your partner, write down the ways in which sarcasm impacts your relationship:

_____

_____

_____

_____

Now write down a way for you and your partner to communicate with one another when sarcasm is occurring, so that neither of you will feel hurt or get upset. _____

_____

* * * * *

Anger

Like many adults with ADD, anger management has been one of the biggest struggles in my life. During the early part of my relationship with my wife, I would frequently be verbally abusive to her. I would either blow up and say hurtful things or I would withdraw in a way that would leave her feeling rejected.

This is a common scenario for couples where one partner has ADD. I have seen the devastating role that anger can play in romantic relationships, as well as family relationships, and friendships.

Poor anger management can do the following:

Cause your partner to feel bad about himself or herself. If you love and care about your partner, then you do not mean to intentionally hurt him or her. After hurting someone you love, you feel pretty rotten about yourself. You may ask yourself, "What is so wrong with me that I keep treating the person I love this way again and again?"

Lead to you blaming your partner for your problems. It is easy to fall into the trap of blaming your partner for your anger. People do not like to feel badly about themselves, whether they have ADD or not.

Degrade the person on the receiving end of your wrath. A person who is repeatedly put down, yelled at, or belittled can't help but think poorly about themselves.

Make your love feel emotionally dead toward you. When people are hurt and put down, yelled at or even hit, then they eventually build an emotional wall around themselves so that they feel nothing. It is very difficult to save a relationship after this has happened.

ADD and Anger

I strongly believe that ADD is a reason for anger, but not an excuse for it. It is true that adults with ADD are more likely to have problems with anger than adults without ADD. Brain scans show that adults with ADD have a decreased level of activity in the prefrontal cortex (of the frontal lobe). This area of the brain is largely responsible for the monitoring of mood and impulse control.

It was a railroad accident that first proved the importance of the frontal lobe in monitoring mood. In 1848 Phineas Gage, a railroad foreman, had a metal bar drilled through his skull, penetrating his frontal cortex. Before the accident Gage had been described as a peaceful, even-tempered man. Afterwards, his personality changed dramatically. He cursed frequently and was angry, stubborn, and impatient.

While individuals with ADD have not experienced the neurological devastation that Phineas Gage suffered, we do have less active frontal lobes. This is why many of us benefit from neurostimulants, which improves our ability to monitor our mood and control our impulses.

The prefrontal cortex can be thought of as our emergency brake. It keeps us from lashing out at others when we feel angry or irritated. When this emergency brake is not functioning properly, it fails to stop us from saying or doing hurtful things.

Owning the Anger Problem

This knowledge does not make us less responsible for our behavior, but more so. If we realize that we have a neurological condition that can cause us to be more angry and impulsive, then we are all the more responsible for being aware of our impulses and keeping them in check.

We must, at some level, believe that we are more than the sum of our parts. We cannot believe that we have an independent will and, at the same time, believe that behavior can solely be explained by biology. We might be able to find genetic, neurological, and biological explanations for why many people are predisposed to certain behaviors, but it cannot explain away all behavior as simply the result of biological or environmental predetermination. We must accept some degree of responsibility for our actions. If we have no control over our behavior, what is the point of reading this book? What is the point of any form of self-directed growth?

For those of us with ADD, luckily we have been blessed with a wonderfully large cerebral cortex (the thinking part of our brains) that can help us gain control of our impulses. We are responsible for thinking before we act, and we experience the consequences of our impulsive behavior and anger, regardless of whether we have a biological explanation for it.

A biological explanation will not make our friends or significant others stay with us or make our employers happier with us when we do a bad job of dealing with people and situations. It will also not change the devastating impact that our anger can have on our family members and romantic life.

What to Do About Your Anger

The question becomes, "If I am going to be responsible for my angry impulses, then what do I do?" You can do the following:

Exercise 12.2

Admit that your anger is your problem and stop blaming others. Until you stop blaming others, or even blaming ADD, and hold yourself personally accountable for the way that you respond to others, you won't make progress. If you feel like a powerless victim, you won't be able to create change in your life. In the space provided, I want you to write down all the excuses you habitually use to blame your spouse, your coworker, your friend, your child, your parent, your past, or whatever, for your anger. I want you to be fully aware that these are not reasons, just excuses: _____

_____

_____

_____

_____

_____

_____

_____

_____

_____

Learn to recognize the physical signs of anger and learn to gain control over your body. When you get angry, what are your bodily reactions? Does your breathing get shallow? Do your jaws tighten? What muscles get tense? Do you clench your fists? Since anger is largely a physiological reaction, if you gain control of your body, you will be a long way toward gaining greater control of your anger. Use the space below to write down what happens to your body when you get angry.

_____

_____

_____

_____

_____

_____

_____

You will need to practice gaining control of these things when you are angry. Many relaxation techniques, like deep breathing, can be helpful in this process. Deep (diaphragmatic) breathing is helpful because it helps relax your body, which takes you out of the body's fight-or-flight response. In other words, it helps take you out of the place where you feel like withdrawing or screaming at someone. You will know that you are breathing correctly by the use of a simple technique. Place one hand on your chest and another on your stomach. Now take a deep breath. If you are breathing from your abdomen, the hand on your stomach will rise and not the hand on your chest. If you are breathing incorrectly, then the reverse will happen. If you have trouble doing this, imagine that you have a Ping-Pong ball in your mouth that you are pulling all the way down to your stomach and then pushing back out slowly. Keep practicing this until you are able to breathe correctly. Whenever you find yourself getting tense or angry, you can use deep breathing as a way of regaining control. (Diaphragmatic breathing techniques are discussed further in chapter 11.)

Learn to approach tense situations in a relaxed manner by disarming your "shoulds." Think of all the different kinds of situations, whether it be dealing with a coworker with whom you do not get along, talking with your spouse or significant other about a sensitive topic, driving in traffic, or dealing with your son being late again, that are likely to make you angry. Describe them. _____

_____

_____

_____

_____

_____

_____

* * * * *

Fighting Absolute Statements

Our anger in situations like the ones you have described are not necessarily triggered by the situations themselves. They are often triggered by the *absolute statements* that we make about those situations. Absolute statements are what we tell ourselves someone else "should" or "should not" do. (See chapter 4 for further discussion.) Remember: *We are not angered by what people do, but by their failure to meet our expectations.* We expect our children to listen to us, for people to drive responsibly, and our spouse or boss to talk to us in a respectful manner. When their behavior does not match that expectation, we become angry.

You might be saying to yourself, "What is this fool talking about? Should we just let people run over us!" Of course I am not saying that. What I am saying is that there is a difference between a hope, or desire, and an expectation. When we have an absolute expectation, versus a hope or desire, we are far more likely to take things personally and respond in an emotional and impulsive manner. Instead of accepting that people are often thoughtless and behave in ways that we do not like, we respond as if they are, with maliciousness and forethought, trying to make our lives miserable.

Here are some facts:

There is no way people are always going to be courteous drivers.

There is no way people are going to always be respectful toward you.

There is no way your kids are always going to tell you the truth or that they are always going to do what you say.

There is no way that everyone is going to always agree with you.

There is no way that people at work are always going to treat you in a respectful or thoughtful manner.

There is no way that life is going to always be fair. If it were then you would probably have a lot less, and starving children in Africa would probably have a lot more.

If you believe otherwise, you will continue to respond to life with anger, bitterness, and resentment.

Exercise 12.3

Now I want you to look back at those situations which are likely to make you angry. What irrational beliefs have helped make you angry and resentful. Write those beliefs down (for example, "Everyone should always drive in a thoughtful and courteous manner").

_____

_____

_____

_____

_____

_____

_____

Now consider what rational beliefs could replace those irrational ones. (For example, "I know I don't like it when someone cuts me off in traffic, but I also know that I am not likely to change that. I am going to choose to remain calm about things I cannot change."

Use the space below to write down some of the rational beliefs you could exchange for some of your irrational beliefs.

_____

_____

_____

_____

_____

_____

Where anger management is concerned, the Serenity Prayer is of great importance. It goes, "God grant me the ability to change the things I can, accept the things I cannot change, and the wisdom to know the difference." If you can live by this principle, you will have a great deal more peace in your life.

Learn to recognize the feelings under your anger. Anger is normally an emotion that masks another emotion. If you can identify what else you are feeling, such as embarrassment or pain, you will find that people will be much more receptive to you.

I can remember a time when I bought my wife a pair of earrings. They were not exactly what she had wanted. I had gone to a great deal of effort to find exactly what she had wanted and felt hurt and disappointed when I did not get the looked-for response from her. My gut reaction was to express anger, but when I curbed this impulse and was able to express that I felt hurt and disappointed, she was able to hear me. This led to a highly productive discussion instead of a fight.

I would like for you to take some time to think about what underlying emotions your anger might cover up. Remember that anger can often feel safer than expressing a more vulnerable part of yourself. What emotions lie underneath the surface of your anger in those situations where your anger is most likely to come out? _____

_____

_____

_____

_____

✳ ✳ ✳ ✳ ✳

The next time you get angry, try to look for those other emotions that lie beneath the surface of your anger. If you can train yourself to express these feelings, rather than your anger, you will find yourself happier in your relationship and in your life.

Chapter 13

The Impact of Listening

Individuals with ADD can focus intensely on things that are of interest to them, almost to the exclusion of anything else. We can, however, find our thoughts jumping from one subject to another when we are dealing with something that is less stimulating. This can have a significant impact on relationships when a non-ADD partner needs to discuss other matters that are important. As Fowler and Fowler (1995) point out, when the non-ADD partner is attempting to get into an in-depth discussion on a topic that is of limited interest to the ADD partner, such as little Johnny's desire for a new pet or house repairs or taxes, the ADD partner's scattered thoughts can be maddening.

Staying on Topic

Your partner and you will need to work out a way to stay on topic when an important issue needs to be addressed. This will help your partner feel less angry, hurt, frustrated, and resentful.

Exercise 13.1

Talk with your spouse or significant other about how the issue of staying on topic impacts your relationship. Give your partner time to talk while you just listen. Use the space below to write down what your partner has said.

_____

_____

_____

_____

Come up with ways that your partner can remind you to stay on topic when you start to drift. Talk about what he or she can say or do that will not offend you. Make a list of these techniques. _____

_____

_____

_____

* * * * *

The Importance of Listening

One of the reasons that my profession is a thriving profession is that people are more than willing to pay money to have someone just listen to them. Many people do not experience this in their daily lives and they desperately want it.

One of the greatest things that you can do for your partner is show your willingness to listen. It communicates to your partner that:

1. You value his or her opinion.

2. You think he or she is important.

3. You care about him or her.

When you are unwilling to listen, it can communicate that:

1. He or she is not important enough for you to take the time to listen.

2. You do not respect your partner or what he or she has to say.

No healthy relationship can exist if one of you does not feel valued and respected by the other. No one feels valued and respected by people who are not willing to listen to what they have to say. If you get nothing else from this workbook, at least understand the extreme importance of taking the time to listen to your partner.

How to Quiet the Mind and Listen

If you follow the next recommendations, you can rest assured that your customers, children, romantic partner, and colleagues will feel more heard and cared for. Your memory will improve because you will be taking the time to slow down and take in information instead of just rushing past it. You will also be able to pick up on a lot of the details in life that you are now missing.

In his book *People Skills*, Dr. Robert Bolton (1979) points out that listening is the combination of hearing what the other person says and suspenseful waiting (an intense psychological involvement with the other). In the process of listening, you are actively immersed in what the other person is saying. To be truly immersed in what someone else is saying, you cannot also be immersed in your own thoughts and interests.

Listening Steps

Take some time to go through the following listening steps with your partner. Let him or her know that you are going to be making a concerted effort to listen. While active listening will become second nature to you over time and, with a lot of practice, will follow effortlessly, it is a good idea to have some help remembering to practice your active listening at first. Your partner will appreciate the effort.

Exercise 13.2

Step One: Limit all other distractions. That means you need to mute the television or cut off the radio. You need to actually turn your attention away from the computer screen. You need to get rid of whatever distractions there are that are going to keep you from being attuned to the person who is speaking.

When a child has trouble paying attention in school, one of the most basic recommendations I make is to move the child close to the front of the class and away from a window or other students who might be a distraction. As as adult, you have to limit your own distractions so that you can pay attention.

Step Two: Take a deep breath, slowly inhaling and exhaling. Quiet your mind and relax. As you breathe out, feel the tension leave your body. If there is anything that you are focusing on, make a quick note to yourself. Now let go of whatever just had your attention, so you can focus your full attention on the person who is speaking.

Step Three: Focus your relaxed gaze on the person who is about to speak.

Step Four: While the other person is speaking, intentionally listen. Do not do the following:

- Think about what you were just doing.

- Think about what you are going to do when the other person has finished talking.

- Think about what you are going to say in response to the other person

- Think about the number of socks with holes in them in your sock drawer.

- Think about your favorite pastime activity.

Simply open your mind to take in what the other person is saying. If you find your mind wandering to other things, simply refocus your attention on the other person.

✳ ✳ ✳ ✳ ✳

Remember that active listening is not a quick technique to learn or an experiment to try out. It is a way of truly being present with your partner. Active listening is not only about your need to pay attention. It is also about your partner's need to feel heard. Like diaphragmatic breathing (see chapter 11), active listening is something that you should practice regularly and often for the rest of your life.

The "How to Get the Other Person Talking" Game

In Dale Carnegie's famous book, *How to Win Friends and Influence People* (1981), he points out that people like to talk about things that interest them. He suggests that you find out what the other person's passion is and get them talking about it.

Of course, Carnegie's main point is that people will like you if you listen to them. But you can also use this technique to improve your listening skills. Treat it as a game. You win if you learn something new from someone else that you did not know before.

If you approach "learning how to listen more and talk less" as a game, it will be more likely to fill your need for stimulation. If you truly listen with the intent of learning more about another person, you will have a great opportunity to develop meaningful friendships and improve how you present yourself to others. You will be shocked by how much smarter you look if you learn to listen more and talk less!

You may wonder what this has to do with your love life, especially if you have been with someone for a long time. You would be surprised at how well it applies. Here are some things couples who have been together ten years or more did not know about each other:

1. A husband did not know his wife had a strong desire to go back to school and become a licensed clinical social worker.

2. A wife did not know that her husband wanted to quit his job and open his own business.

3. A life partner did not know that his live-in lover of ten years wanted to become a pilot. He later became one with the support of his lover and their relationship dramatically improved.

Few things can have such a positive impact on a relationship as helping a partner fulfill his or her heart's desire. I know how close I felt to my wife when she supported me in writing this book and in believing that I could do it. I also know how much it has meant to her that she has my full support in going to dental school. There can be sheer joy in watching your spouse blossom. What a wonderful gift to have someone who is willing to support you, listen to you, and believe in you.

Chapter 14

ADD and Sexual Intimacy

ADD has such a strong influence on other aspects of romantic relationships, it only makes sense that it can also have an impact on our sexual relationships. The most obvious way that ADD can hurt sexual intimacy is by helping to create emotional distance.

How ADD Creates Distance

ADD symptoms can help create emotional distance in the following ways:

1. The non-ADD partner feels unheard because of the ADD partner's poor listening skills.

2. The non-ADD partner feels unimportant because the ADD partner hyperfocuses on other things.

3. The non-ADD partner feels hurt and angry because of angry outbursts and irritability on the part of the ADD partner.

4. The non-ADD partner feels resentful about things that the ADD partner has not taken care of and/or is tired of feeling responsible for most things.

5. The ADD partner feels nagged by the non-ADD partner and does not want to be around him or her.

6. The ADD partner is no longer stimulated by the non-ADD partner and, thus, feels no longer "in love."

What to Do to Increase Sexual Intimacy

In *Adventures in Fast Forward*, Kathleen Nadeau (1996) has some very good recommendations for dealing with sexual intimacy problems in relationships when there is an ADD partner:

1. Relax together. Many adults with ADD can become very tense and preoccupied. We have difficulty unwinding. Nadeau suggests that bathing and showering together, meditating together, or massaging one another can help to create an environment conducive to sexual intimacy.

2. Get away together. Because distractibility and preoccupation are constant companions for adults with ADD, brief getaways can help you focus on your partner and help the two of you reconnect. "ADD adults who are prone to rush through sexual relations, leaving their partner feeling unsatisfied, may be able to slow down and enjoy a more prolonged sensual experience away from the pressure and distractions of daily living." (85)

3. Be adventurous. Restlessness and rapid boredom are facts of life for some people with ADD. "No matter how attractive or interesting a . . . partner may be, an ADD adult may find himself feeling dissatisfied." (85) This brings to light the importance of variety and spontaneity for many adults with ADD. Of course, any adventurous sex is something that needs to be comfortable to both partners. Nadeau adds, "It is crucial that the non-ADD spouse realize that this need for added stimulation is not a reflection on him or her, but is a built-in aspect of the partner's ADD." (85)

4. Communicate honestly. This next point, in my opinion, is one of the most vital points. Nadeau points out that "an ADD partner, in particular, may need more direct communication because he or she may not pick up as readily on more subtle cues." (85) Non-ADD partners may feel, at times, that they are being direct and that the ADD partner is just not getting the point. But if the ADD partner is not getting the point, then the non-ADD partner needs to be more direct. The non-ADD partner needs to be sensitive, but as direct as possible.

5. Be honest about how you want to be touched. Nadeau states, "Rhythmic stroking, which might be considered soothing or sexual to some people, may feel annoying or irritating to some ADD adults. Such reactions need to be expressed matter-of-factly so that they do not become misinterpreted as 'you don't want me to touch you' by the non-ADD spouse." (85)

For the non-ADD partner:

6. Learn to recognize ADD patterns and not misinterpret them. Nadeau cites an example of an ADD individual who got so hyperfocused on the computer that it got in the way of intimacy between him and his spouse. She shows that through

ADD-focused counseling, the wife was able to recognize that this was an ADD tendency and not about her. They were then able to work on solutions to deal with the problem.

I have a few more suggestions to add to this list.

Make it just about the other person at times. I have found that it helps to do things with intentionality. If you have a tendency to hyperfocus on things at times, then why not choose to hyperfocus on the sexual and intimacy needs of your love? Is it not true that creativity is one of the positive hallmarks of ADD? Why not try to use that creativity to make your love happy and sexually fulfilled? The creative aspect will fill your need for stimulation, and your love will feel cared for and special because of the attention and focus she or he receives.

Schedule loving gestures. This recommendation is geared more toward men with ADD. You may very well have heard that "men give intimacy to get sex and women give sex to get intimacy." There is a large amount of truth to this. No matter how understanding your female lover is, if she does not feel connected to you, over time your sex life will suffer. To have a healthy sex life, you need to have regular patterns of connection that become a habit. Here are some ideas:

- Make it a habit to kiss your love and take some time for her when you come home from work.

- Schedule time together when the focus is just to talk and be with one another. Make this time sacrosanct. (If you do not make it sacrosanct—if you get on the computer, or find other reasons not to have your scheduled time together—you will make your love feel even less important.)

- Mark randomly in your calendar times to do something thoughtful for your love. It is often a good idea to put these random prompts in your calendar at the beginning of the year.

- Use your calendar to remember important dates. Nothing can make someone feel less important than forgetting their birthday or a wedding anniversary or, if you are not married, the anniversary of your first date.

- Look for times that you could show a thoughtful gesture. If your love calls and says that she is hungry then let her know that you will be picking her up and taking her out for dinner or that you will be bringing something home. Make it a surprise that you know she will like.

Exercise 14.1

Adults with ADD are not always the greatest at picking up on the details, and these details are incredibly important in communicating to your love that you care. It can help to develop a relationship "cheat sheet."

This exercise will probably be more helpful to you if you are a man. Let's face it, most men *without* ADD have enough trouble paying attention to their partners. If you are a man with attention deficit disorder, then your difficulty attending to your partner is compounded.

Fill in the missing information on the next few pages. Take your time with it. The process of gathering the information can be as helpful to your relationship as having the information. It can be a way of opening up some good discussion with your partner and drawing you closer together.

When your partner wants to go out to eat it will mean a whole lot more if you have taken the time to "think" about what he or she would like rather than just saying "wherever you would like to go." Also, if you are willing to make the reservations, it will show you care.

This information will be handy in purchasing gifts and will show that you know your partner's tastes.

Favorite Colors

Clothing or Accessories (Might be different for different seasons and can change from year to year depending on fashion)	1._____ 2._____ 3._____
For the Home (Might be different for different rooms in the home. Look at what your partner has already chosen and duplicate or find complementary colors).	1._____ 2._____ 3._____

The next table breaks down gifts into four different groups based on financial cost. It lists:

1. Things that have no financial cost. This group includes things that cost you little more than your time. These should be thoughtful, considerate, and loving gestures, such as coming home early to spend some extra time with your partner, or watching the kids to give your partner some time off.

2. Things that have little financial cost. These are little gestures that do not cost much but say "I love you." They can include bringing home flowers, or surprising your partner at the office with some take-out food for lunch.

3. Things that have moderate financial cost. What constitutes moderate to significant financial cost will depend on your current station in life. This would involve things that you could not afford to do more than one time per week to one time per month without it pinching the budget. For a middle-class family, it might be going to a concert or a nice dinner.

4. Things that have significant financial cost. This involves things that you would not do more than a couple of times a year. It might be purchasing a new piece of furniture that your partner has been wanting or a print by your partner's favorite artist. It could also involve buying tickets for that vacation he or she has always wanted. For these gifts it is good to know what she is passionate about.

It is important to note that the emotional value of a gift is certainly not tied to the financial cost of that gift. I remember a story the assistant pastor of my childhood church once told me. Dr. Ryan, my assistant pastor, was also a chaplain in the Army reserves. One year, upon returning home from his monthly weekend duty, he realized that he had forgotten all about his wife's birthday. He did not have time to go out and get her a gift before he saw her, but he took the time to make her a card. He wrote "Bang!" twenty-one times on the card, and then wrote, "I am sorry that all I have for you right now is this card because you deserve a 21-gun salute!" The card meant so much to her that she kept it years after the fact.

List some possible gifts in the spaces provided:

Price Range	Gift
No Cost	_____
No Cost	_____
No Cost	_____
No Cost	_____
Little Cost	_____
Little Cost	_____
Little Cost	_____
Little Cost	_____
Moderate Cost	_____
Moderate Cost	_____
Moderate Cost	_____
Moderate Cost	_____
Significant Cost	_____
Significant Cost	_____
Significant Cost	_____
Significant Cost	_____

It is important to know what helps your love to relax. If you are able to learn to recognize when your partner is tense, then you will be able to show that you care.

Times My Love Is Most Tense or Uptight	What Would Help My Love Relax

Certain conversation starters can help you explore your love's inner self. This will help your partner feel more connected with you on a deeper level. Make sure that you have the time to listen and be attentive. Be sensitive and only talk about what your love wants to discuss: When discussing these topics, it is very important to use good listening skills and truly express an interest. It is also important that you listen without judgment. Choose a topic from the following list.

- happiest childhood memory
- most painful childhood memory
- first childhood memory
- best memory of the two of you together
- what a perfect day would be like
- dreams of the future
- greatest fear
- what you value in him or her and what he or she values in you
- perfect sexual experience
- what gives life meaning (if nothing does, then what would?)
- what makes her (him) feel loved and respected

* * * * *

Sex is sometimes, unfortunately, very difficult for some couples to talk about. It is important that you learn to talk openly about sex together if you want to know how to best satisfy your lover's needs and if you want your needs satisfied to the best of your lover's ability. You can use the following exercise as a way of getting to know each other better.

Exercise 14.2

Find a time that is calm and relaxing for each of you so that you can give this exercise the focus it deserves. You do not have to do this in one sitting. In fact, it might be good to set aside multiple times. You might work on it in bed together before you go to sleep at night.

Once again, the ADD partner needs to practice good listening skills. It is often good to write down what your partner is saying because then you are more likely to listen rather than be formulating your own response. Apart from asking probing questions, you need to just listen.

It is also important to note that when you talk about sex, you are talking about a lot more than just intercourse. You are talking about what makes you attracted to one another. You are talking about what makes you relaxed and receptive to sexual activity. You are talking about foreplay and all that means to you. You are talking about touch, safety, likes, dislikes, and the myriad of other things that are part of the sexual dance between humans. Before discussing the questions below, let your love know that there will be no expectation of doing something that will make him or her feel uncomfortable. Also, don't let things roll off the frontal lobe that will be offensive to your love. With this in mind, each of you should answer the questions on the following pages.

What I need to physically and emotionally feel relaxed and receptive sexually is:

My Response	My Partner's Response

What makes me feel sexually excited/stimulated the most is:

My Response	My Partner's Response

The way I liked to be touched sexually is:

My Response	My Partner's Response

What I enjoy the most about sex is:

My Response	My Partner's Response

My fantasy sexual experience would involve (remember to not say anything that would be offensive to your love):

My Response	My Partner's Response

What makes me feel uncomfortable sexually is (be willing to listen without defensiveness):

My Response	My Partner's Response

What I enjoy most about our sexual experiences is (be constructive):

My Response	My Partner's Response

What would make my sex life even better would be (don't say things that would make your love feel uncomfortable or that would be offensive):

My Response	My Partner's Response

✳ ✳ ✳ ✳ ✳

The purpose of this chapter has been to help you and your partner get to know one another physically and emotionally at a deeper level. ADD can, at times, get in the way of understanding your partner's sexual and emotional needs, but if you are willing to make a concerted effort to become aware of who your partner is and what your partner needs, you can be a more caring, loving, and thoughtful mate.

Chapter 15

Social Blunders, Poor Boundaries, and Impulsiveness

Individuals with ADD can sometimes have a tendency to talk too much or say inappropriate things. Your love might also not want everyone else to know what is going on in your personal life. A funeral might not be a good place to tell a joke and when the preacher is visiting might not be a good time to tell a dirty joke.

Harley and Annie's Story

Harley was a friend of mine who also had ADD. Harley had no idea how incredibly inappropriate he was. It was obvious that this was incredibly uncomfortable for his wife, Annie. She was a relatively private person and she did not want the world to know about her sex life or every argument they had. She would also get embarrassed when Harley would tell dirty jokes and use the "F" word even when children were around. It became so uncomfortable for her that they quit going out or doing much together.

The fact of the matter was that Harley's behavior was so outrageous that a lot of his friends, including myself, quit having much to do with him. A good example of how outrageous his behavior could be was shared by the wife of a friend. She apparently went over to Harley and Annie's house soon after Harley had surgery. She happened to be a nurse. Because of this, Harley did not see the problem in dropping his pants in front of her and showing her the stitches where his right testicle used to be.

While, I must admit, there were times I found Harley funny, it got to the point that it was too painful to see the impact that his outrageous behavior had on his wife. It was just difficult to be around Harley after a while. Behavior that used to have some degree of humor to it just became annoying, and even insulting, after a while. Even though I knew Harley did not intend to be insulting and inappropriate, and I had some degree of sympathy for him, it was just not worth it. His behavior was too outlandish, and he obviously was not going to gain the insight necessary to change. Whenever anyone confronted him about his behavior, he would just become angry and accuse others, including his wife of abusing and victimizing him.

While most of us will not drop our pants and show our privates to a friend's spouse, we often tend to act in ways that make our loves feel uncomfortable at times. These might include:

- Forgetting the personal connections between various people and saying the wrong thing to the wrong person

- Telling off-color jokes at inappropriate times

- Being unintentionally insulting to others by saying something insensitive (due to not thinking before speaking)

- Not respecting the personal space of others

- Talking too much and too loudly

- Forgetting to acknowledge or introduce your partner

- Ignoring your partner

- Asking people you hardly know over to your house or trying to make plans with people you hardly know even when they obviously are not comfortable with such an invitation

- Bragging or talking about yourself too much

When you are capable of doing so in a calm manner without getting upset, be willing to have an open and frank discussion with your partner about if and how this kind of behavior has impacted your relationship.

Exercise 15.1

You can come up with some subtle ways for your spouse to let you know when you are being inappropriate when the two of you are in public. Such subtle cues can save both of you from embarrassment. Remember, if you care for your spouse or significant other, you should be willing to work on this. You will be willing to learn to edit yourself better with your partner's assistance. Use the space below to take notes on what you discuss.

_____

_____

_____

✳ ✳ ✳ ✳ ✳

Impulsive Spending

If you are an ADD adult who has issues with impulsivity, impulsive spending is one of the most negative ways that your impulsiveness can impact a committed relationship. If you spend money on impulse, it can lead to frequent conflicts with your partner. If your partner needs to feel financially secure, and doesn't because of your impulsive spending, then your partner is going to have a whole storehouse of negative feelings toward you.

I have found that more relationships end over money issues than anything else, including infidelity. While money can clearly represent prestige and freedom, it can also represent safety and security. While the full emotional, relational, psychological, and spiritual ramifications of money easily fall well beyond the scope of this workbook, it is important to say that impulsive spending habits can lead to:

- Resentment in both partners. The non-ADD partner, who is often less impulsive with money, might resent that the ADD partner is spending money too freely. The ADD partner might feel resentment if he or she feels "controlled and restricted" by his or her partner's money concerns.

- The non-ADD partner might feel like he or she has to function as the parent for the ADD partner. He or she might feel in the position of saying "yes" or "no" to expenditures when he or she would like to be able to make joint decisions on finances.

- If both partners have problems controlling impulsive spending, then they might get into serious financial problems. This lays the ground for long-term, chronic stress. It can cause anger, anxiety, fights, and even increase the likelihood of physical abuse and substance abuse.

- If the ADD partner buys a great deal of things for himself or herself without thinking about his or her partner's wants and needs, then the non-ADD partner can feel uncared for.

Fowler and Fowler (1995) point out that "ADD people have to treat money with the care that everyone else gives it, only more so. That is, they follow the same rules as non-ADD folk, but they have to make the rules even more stringent and follow them more closely" (119). Their suggestions include:

- **Don't allow indebtedness.** Avoid credit card debt by paying your balance each month and generally not buying things unless you can pay cash. (I personally feel that this is a good principle for everyone, no matter if they have ADD or not.)

- **Have a twenty-four to forty-eight hour rule.** This just means that you don't buy on impulse. You make an agreement with yourself to wait a certain period of time before you allow your impulsivity to get you stuck with a purchase you will wind up neither wanting nor needing. If you don't think you can follow this rule, at least agree to save the receipt and not use the purchase for twenty-four to forty-eight hours so that you have the option of returning it after the desire for the object has passed.

- **Shop around.** Don't buy that car or lawn mower or piece of furniture the first place you go to. See if you can get a better deal somewhere else.

- **Ask yourself if this purchase is really going to make you as happy as you think it will.** Some people are notorious for buying things that they think are wonderful only to find that they are simply adding useless clutter to their lives. If you have a tendency to do this, then remember to stop and evaluate whether the item you are about to purchase will actually add any quality to your life or serve any purpose.

- **Develop a budget and commit to following it.** People with ADD can be good at developing budgets. After all, it can be fun to plan and think about things. The real problem comes in sticking with a budget. If you want it to work, you must commit to following it even when your instinct is telling you otherwise.

In addition to these recommendations, I also suggest the use of a checkbook instead of cash or a credit card. Not only does using a checkbook slow down the purchasing process, thus decreasing the likelihood of an impulse buy, but it also helps you keep better track of your money. When you can see your bank account balance dropping, you will be more likely to pay attention. Of course, if you use your checkbook like this, then it is vitally important that you keep good records in your checkbook register.

Exercise 15.2

If you are an impulsive spender, answer the following questions in the spaces provided. How has impulsive behavior in relation to money caused problems for you? How has it hampered paying bills, saving for retirement, being in a relationship, or having a general sense of well-being? _____

_____

_____

_____

_____

What excuses (e.g., "I deserve it" or "I just have to have it") do you make when you are impulsive with your spending? What excuses will you agree not to make anymore? _____

_____

_____

_____

What changes are you going to make to gain greater control over your money and your impulsive spending? _____

_____

_____

_____

_____

✳ ✳ ✳ ✳ ✳

Money concerns are a good thing to discuss with your romantic partner, especially if you are married and/or have children together. To have a successful long-term relationship, you have to have some workable agreements on money issues. If the two of you cannot seem to work it out together, then I would suggest meeting with a financial planner.

Chapter 16

The Love Bank

I read about the concept of the Love Bank in Steven Covey's *The Seven Habits of Highly Effective People* (1989). I must say that I have found it to be one of the most useful concepts in working with couples, regardless of whether one of the partners has ADD or not.

Just imagine your relationship has an emotional bank account. Every time you forget to do something you said you would do, or forget to say thank you, or forget to be considerate, or get caught up in your work or latest interest and forget your partner, or leave piles of stuff around the house without picking it up, or get irritated and upset and say hurtful things, or just say something thoughtless, you make an emotional withdrawal from your bank account.

In his book *ADD and Romance* (1998), Jonathan Scott Halverstadt does a marvelous job of pointing out the positive and negative impacts of ADD on romantic relationships. The following sums up his list of the negative ways that a partner can feel as a result of the behavior of an individual with ADD.

1. "He's just not there for me!" (The ADD partner is not fully present emotionally and/or intellectually). If you are focused on several things at once, you cannot be fully present for your partner. This can cause your partner to feel very uncared for.

2. "She does not think before she acts or speaks!" The ADD partner impulsively:

   - Butts in on conversations

   - Spends money

   - Says hurtful things without thinking of the consequences

3. "He would forget his head if it were not tied on!" The ADD partner is:

   - Late, or totally forgets, plans and commitments
   - Forgets to pay bills
   - Forgets important dates

4. "She never finishes anything she starts!" The ADD partner exhibits poor follow-through.

5. "He is always leaving stuff lying around everywhere!" This is self-explanatory.

6. "I love her, but she is the most disorganized person I know!" Ditto.

7. "But you said you loved me!" The ADD partner has difficulty staying on task, including staying on task in a relationship. Just about the time the relationship begins to grow to a deeper level, the ADD partner may become bored, so that he or she spends less time focused on the relationship. This can cause both partners to feel that love has faded.

8. "I say black, she says white." The ADD partner is argumentative, conflict-seeking.

9. "He has a one-track mind." The ADD partner hyperfocuses.

10. "She is so incredibly inconsiderate!" All of the above characteristics are combined into one person. He or she:

    - does not follow through with commitments;
    - gets bored with things that are important to his or her partner;
    - gets stuck in obsessive thinking;
    - is disorganized;
    - is forgetful;
    - is routinely late;
    - is argumentative.

These issues can obviously cause some major withdrawals in your relationship's emotional bank account. If you are not making some intentional love investments, then your relationship will be emotionally bankrupt before you know it!

It does not take roses and a violin player. An emotional investment is simply any expression to your partner, in a positive and thoughtful way, that he or she is important in your life. Small things that can count as an emotional investment can include the following:

- Doing your part around the house without being asked

- Noticing any time that your sweetheart is under stress and offering to help without being asked

- Giving a backrub without expectation of reciprocity

- Sending an e-mail for no reason

- Bringing home flowers or a card just to say "I love you"

- Leaving a note

- Going grocery shopping or doing some other routine activity with your spouse or partner just to be with him or her

- Giving a call just to say hello

- Giving up that Monday night football game just because you want to spend time with your partner

- Offering to pick up the kids on your way home

- Remembering to ask your sweetheart if he or she wants something to drink when you get up to get something for yourself

- Noticing his or her new haircut

- Remembering to give him or her a kiss when you come home

- Being willing to share the details of your day even when you do not feel like it

- Establishing and keeping a special time to spend with one another

If you have ADD then you can bet that your emotional withdrawals are going to be consistent. You better do something to make sure your emotional investments are also consistent if you want to have a good relationship. The key to love investments is that they are something that you do, regardless of whether you feel like it, on a regular basis to express to your partner that he or she is significant in your life. If you only invest when you feel like it, then the concept will be of no use to you. It has to become a habit. Here are some suggestions:

- Put up a sticky note where you can easily see it to remind you to make your love investments

- Put prompts in your appointment book on a regular basis

- Make a clear commitment to make a love investment every day until it becomes a habit

- Set aside regular appointments with your partner that you commit to not breaking

- Become alert to the signs that your partner is being neglected. Be willing to meet his or her needs without responding defensively. Learn to value those needs as much as your own.

Exercise 16.1

In the space provided, write down the major ways in which you make withdrawals from the emotional bank account of your relationship: _____

_____

_____

_____

_____

Write down some things that you can do to reduce your current emotional withdrawals:

_____

_____

_____

_____

Write down your current emotional investments in this relationship: _____

_____

_____

_____

Write down ways in which you would like to improve on those emotional investments:

_____

_____

_____

_____

Write down new emotional investments that you would like to make (things that you would like to start doing): _____

_____

_____

_____

_____

* * * * *

Chapter 17

ADD and Medications

There is not doubt that for individuals with ADD, medication can have a positive impact. According to Dr. Daniel G. Amen (2001), appropriate goals for medication include:

1. decreased distractibility

2. decreased restlessness

3. decreased impulsiveness

4. increased thoughtfulness

5. decreased irritability

6. increased motivation

7. improved interpersonal functioning

The Positive Impact of Medications

I have frequently seen medications help relationships in the following ways:

Reducing the "open mouth and insert foot" phenomenon. Medication will often help adults with ADD stop and think before speaking. This can decrease our tendency to say hurtful things, make social blunders, and just say things without thinking in general.

Reducing the tendency to argue for the sake of arguing. Stimulation is self-medication for adults with ADD. With neurostimulant medication, the need to have external stimulation is decreased and, along with it, picky behavior and argumentativeness.

Increasing the ability to listen. The ability to pay attention to others and what is going on is often greatly increased on medication.

Increasing ability to organize. Medications can help an ADD adult remember to think through the steps of what needs to be done, instead of just doing things without thinking. This also helps our ability to put away things. The house will often become less cluttered when an ADD adult goes on medication.

Increasing the ability to sit down and just "be" with someone. Neurostimulant medication can often decrease feelings of restlessness. This makes it easier for the ADD partner to sit down and spend quality time with a partner.

Decreasing irritation. ADD adults on medication often report feeling less overwhelmed by life in general. They often report that they find it easier to deal with the frustrations that life brings without becoming irritated. This can obviously be a welcome change in a relationship.

Increasing thoughtfulness. In short, an ADD adult on medication often just remembers to be thoughtful. Instead of jumping from thought to thought, or just being caught up with whatever is happening, it becomes easier to stop and think about what the other person might want or need. This can obviously help in making our partners feel more significant and cared for.

Medication to Treat ADD

Various medications and medication groups are used to treat ADD. In the next section, I first cover neurostimulant medications, which are the most commonly used; Ritalin, the best-known medication treatment for ADD, belongs to this group. Then I cover some other types of medications that are also used to treat ADD.

Neurostimulant Medications

In Amen's opinion, Adderall and Concerta are the most preferable of the neurostimulant medications. They last longer than regular-release Ritalin and Dexedrine (five to seven hours for Adderall and ten to eleven hours for Concerta, versus two to four hours for regular-release Ritalin and Dexedrine). Both are generally taken one to two times daily and are smoother in taking effect and wearing off (Amen 2001). Amen also points out that Adderall is broken down into four strengths and that the Adderall tablet is double-scored so that it can be halved and quartered, to fine-tune the dose.

Since last year, a sustained-release version of Adderall, called Adderall XR, has become available. The sustained-release version of this medication is supposed to stay in the body approximately two hours longer. In other words, the sustained-release version of Adderall should stay in your system seven to nine hours instead of five to seven hours.

Benefits of stimulant medication, include the following:

- improved attention span

- decreased distractibility

- increased ability to finish tasks

- improved ability to follow directions

- decreased hyperactivity and restlessness

- lessened impulsivity

- improved handwriting (Amen 2001)

I personally take Adderall and have found it to be highly helpful. I find that when I am on the medication, I

- get paper work done;

- keep my office clean and orderly;

- stay on a single task to completion;

- listen more and talk less;

- have less of a sense of restlessness;

- can generally follow the recommendations outlined in this book more effectively.

Effexor and SSRI Medications

In *Healing ADD* (Amen 2001), he discusses six subtypes of ADD. One of the subtypes he discusses is overfocused ADD. Individuals who have this subtype will often get so intensely focused on one thing, whether it be something that they are doing, or something that they want, or a topic that interests them, that it is extremely difficult for them to let go of the topic or interest, to refocus on something else.

SSRIs (selective serotonin reuptake inhibitors), such as Paxil, Prozac, or Zoloft, can help a person who overfocuses. But they can, as a side effect, hinder a person's ability to focus or concentrate on other things.

Dr. Amen recommends Effexor, which increases both serotonin and dopamine (a neurostimulant). If the person with overfocused ADD does not respond well to Effexor, he or she should be placed on both an SSRI and a neurostimulant at the same time (Amen 2001).

Anti-Convulsant Medications

For people with aggression problems, mood instability, and headaches, anti-convulsant medication, combined with a neurostimulant, may help (Amen 2001). Examples of anti-convulsant medications include Carbatrol, valproic acid, Depakote, and Neurontin.

Anti-Depressant Medication with Neurostimulant Qualities

The following anti-depressant medications are also used to treat ADD: Norpramin, Tofranil, Wellbutrin and Wellbutrin SR, Elavil, and Sinequan. These medications work by increasing the neurotransmitters norepinephrine and dopamine. I am most familiar with Wellbutrin and Wellbutrin SR. Many of the doctors with whom I work will prescribe Wellbutrin when there appear to be both symptoms of ADD and depression.

As can be seen, there are a variety of medication options available to treat ADD. If you are considering medications, it would be worthwhile to find a psychiatrist or neurologist who is very familiar with the diagnosis and treatment of adult ADD. You may want to use the ADDA Web site or Dr. Amen's Web site (see appendix D) to find a qualified neurologist or psychiatrist.

Chapter 18

Wrapping Up

This book is about making changes to improve your relationship. It is important to remember, as you make positive changes, to communicate with your partner appropriately. It is important to incorporate your partner in the change process and to talk with him or her openly about what you are doing. Otherwise, there is too much room for misunderstandings. For instance, when I started taking greater responsibility for my morning routine, I would frequently get angry at my wife for going through the "have you done" and "do you have" lists with me. After all, I was seeing her as standing in the way of my self-imposed interventions. She, in turn, felt hurt and rejected. When we sat down and talked about what I was doing and I included her in the process, she felt better and so did I.

Changing the Rules

If you are going to change the way that things have been established for years, then you have to let your partner know. After probably being exposed to a mountain of self-help information through books and talk shows, we should all get the point that open communication is important.

Exercise 18.1

Now that you have finished this workbook, what changes are you thinking of making and how can you openly discuss those changes with your partner in a non-threatening manner? _____

_____

_____

_____

_____

_____

What needs of your partner need to be considered before making changes? For instance, you might want to take on more responsibility, but there are certain things that your partner is more comfortable doing by him or herself. _____

_____

_____

What kinds of things will the two of you need to compromise on? _____

_____

_____

In what ways can your partner be used as a support for these changes? In what ways does he or she want to be included? _____

_____

_____

_____

_____

✳ ✳ ✳ ✳ ✳

Exercise 18.2

Early on in this workbook, you wrote down the positive changes you would be able to observe in yourself and others by the time you finished reading it. Now that you have finished this workbook, what positive changes are observable? Write those positive changes below: _____

_____

_____

_____

What is your plan to make those changes stick? How are you going to make those changes positive habits in your life for the long haul? For instance, if you plan on being more thoughtful, are you going to use visual prompts in your calendar to remind yourself to be thoughtful? _____

_____

_____

_____

What changes do you still want to make? _____

_____

_____

_____

How do you plan to make those changes? Be specific. _____

_____

_____

_____

In what ways has your romantic partner observed positive changes in you and what is his or her response to those changes? _____

_____

_____

_____

What have you learned from this workbook that you do not want to forget? _____

_____

_____

_____

_____

_____

* * * * *

Appendix A

Diagnostic and Statistical Manual (DSM-IV) Criteria for ADHD

A. Either (1) or (2):

(1) six (or more) of the following symptoms of inattention have persisted for at least six months to a degree that is maladaptive and inconsistent with developmental level:

Inattention

(a) often fails to give close attention to details or makes careless mistakes in schoolwork, work, or other activities

(b) often has difficulty sustaining attention in tasks or play activities

(c) often does not seem to listen to what is being said to him or her

(d) often does not follow through on instructions and fails to finish schoolwork, chores, or duties in the workplace (not due to oppositional behavior or failure to understand instructions)

(e) often has difficulty organizing tasks and activities

(f) often avoids or strongly dislikes tasks (e.g., schoolwork or homework) that require sustained mental effort

(g) often loses things necessary for activities

(h) is often easily distracted by extraneous stimuli

(i) is often forgetful in daily activities

(2) six (or more) of the following symptoms of hyperactivity-impulsivity have persisted for at least 6 months to a degree that is maladaptive and inconsistent with developmental level:

Hyperactive

(a) often fidgets with hands or feet and squirms in seat

(b) often leaves seat in classroom or in other situations in which remaining seated is expected

(c) often runs about or climbs excessively in situations where it is inappropriate (in adolescents or adults, may be limited to subjective feelings of restlessness)

(d) often has difficulty playing or engaging in leisure activities quietly

(e) is often "on the go" or often acts as if "driven by a motor"

(f) often talks excessively

Impulsivity

(g) often blurts out answers to questions before the questions have been completed

(h) often has difficulty awaiting turn

B. Onset no later than age 7.

C. Symptoms must be present in 2 or more situations (e.g., at school, work, and at home).

D. The disturbance causes clinically significant distress or impairment in social, academic, or occupational functioning.

E. Does not occur exclusively during the course of a psychotic disorder (e.g., schizophrenia) and is not better accounted for by mood, anxiety, dissociative, or personality disorder. (APA 2000, 92–93)

Appendix B

Questions to Ask Medical and Mental Health Professionals

Name of Professional: _____

1. How long have you been treating adults with ADHD? _____

_____

_____

2. What percentage of your current caseload is made up of adults with ADHD? _____

_____

_____

3. What kind of continuing education involving adult ADHD have you been involved in?

_____

_____

_____

4. Are you familiar with Children and Adults with Attention Deficit Disorders (CHADD or the National Attention Deficit Disorders Association (ADDA)? Circle YES or NO.

5. Have you given presentations or written any articles on adult ADHD? Circle YES or NO.

6. What books related to adult ADHD are you familiar with? _____

_____

_____

Appendix C

Questions for Your Parents

Did your mom or dad have trouble concentrating or focusing in school or was school particularly difficult for either one of them? If yes, what kinds of problems? _____

_____

_____

Did any of your siblings have any particular problems with concentration and focus or any particular difficulties in school? Do any of them suffer from a mental health or substance abuse problem? _____

_____

_____

List the family members on your father's side of the family who had the following problems:

Depression or suicidal behavior: _____

Anxiety or panic attacks: _____

Substance abuse problems: _____

Psychotic disorders: _____

Epilepsy or other neurological problems: _____

Tic disorders: _____

ADD or problems in school: _____

Anger problems: _____

Legal problems: _____

List any members on your mother's side of the family who have had the following problems:

Depression or suicidal behavior: _____

Anxiety or panic attacks: _____

Substance abuse problems: _____

Psychotic disorders: _____

Epilepsy or other neurological problems: _____

Tic disorders: _____

ADD or problems in school: _____

Anger problems: _____

Legal problems: _____

Is there any history of head trauma you experienced as a child? If so, what was it and when was it? _____

Did your mom experience any physical trauma during pregnancy with you? _____

_____

Were there any complications during delivery with you? _____

How well did you get your homework done as a kid? _____

Were you hyperactive as a kid? _____

How well did you follow rules and do as you were told? _____

Did you have trouble losing things and keeping track of things? _____

Did you have particular difficulty keeping yourself organized as a kid? _____

_____

In elementary school how well were you accepted by other children? _____

_____

Were there any subjects you had particular difficulty with? _____

What would your teachers say about you? _____

How easy were you to get up in the morning and get to bed at night? _____

Did you have many temper tantrums or anger outbursts as a kid? If so, what would trigger them? _____

_____

Did you have particular problems listening or paying attention as a kid? _____

Appendix D

Professional and Self-Help Resources

Self-Help Books

Healing ADD: The Breakthrough Program That Allows You to Heal the Six Types of ADD, by D. G. Amen. New York: G. P. Putnam's Sons, 2001.
No matter how many books you have read on ADD, this book will enhance your knowledge and understanding. It clearly explains the neurology behind ADD and gives practical and useful suggestions.

ADD and Romance, by J. Halverstadt. Dallas, Tex.: Taylor Publishing Co., 1998.
This is a well-written book that also addresses the issues of ADD and romantic relationships. If you are interested in gaining another perspective on the positive and negative ramifications of ADD on relationships, this would be a very good book to consider.

Living with ADD: A Workbook for Adults with Attention Deficit Disorder, by M. S. Roberts and G. J. Jansen. Oakland, Calif.: New Harbinger Publications, 1997.
This book addresses other personal and interpersonal issues related to ADD.

Adventures in Fast Forward: Life, Love, and Work for the ADD Adult, by K. G. Nadeau. New York: Brunner/Mazel Publishers, 1996.
This is a very user-friendly book. If you read this book, you will come away with some very useful strategies for dealing with life, love, and work. It has an excellent resource list.

Happiness Is a Serious Problem: A Human Nature Repair Manual, by D. Prager. New York: Regan Books, 1998.
   This book is not about ADD, but the topics that it covers are so universal that I have cited it several times in this workbook. Everyone would benefit from reading this book.

Organizations

The National Attention Deficit Disorders Association (ADDA)
1788 Second St., Suite 200
Highland Park, IL 60035
Phone: 847-432-2332
www.add.org

Children and Adults with Attention Deficit Disorder (CHADD)
8181 Professional Place, Suite 201
Landover, MD 20785
Phone: 800-233-4050
www.chadd.com

Narcotics Anonymous (NA)
P.O. Box 9999
Van Nuys, CA 91409
Phone: 818-773-9999
www.na.org

Alcoholics Anonymous (AA)
AA General Services Office
475 Riverside Drive
New York, NY 10015
Phone: 212-870-3400
www.alcoholics-anonymous.org

Web Sites

www.personalitypathways.com
   This Web page will help you find out more about the Myers-Briggs Type Indicator (MBTI).

www.amenclinic.com
   This is Dr. Daniel Amen's Web site. It is filled with useful information.

www.flylady.net
   This Web site is clearly geared toward women, but I think it would be helpful for anyone who is having difficulty keeping his or her home clean and organized.

References

APA (American Psychiatric Association). 2000. *Diagnostic and Statistical Manual of Mental Disorders.* Fourth edition. Text Revision. Washington, D.C.: American Psychiatric Association.

Amen, D. G. 2001. *Healing ADD: The Breakthrough Program That Allows You to Heal the Six Types of ADD.* New York: G. P. Putnam's Sons.

Benson, H. 1975. *The Relaxation Response.* New York: William Morrow.

Bolton, R. 1979. *People Skills: How to Assert Yourself, Listen to Others, and Resolve Conflicts.* New York: Simon and Schuster.

Carnegie, D. 1981. *How to Win Friends and Influence People.* Revised edition. New York: Simon and Schuster.

Caudill, M. A. 1995. *Managing Pain Before It Manages You.* New York: Guilford Press.

Covey, S. R. 1989. *The Seven Habits of Highly Effective People.* New York: Simon and Schuster.

Fowler, R., and J. Fowler. 1995. *Honey, Are You Listening?: How Attention Deficit Disorder Could Be Affecting Your Marriage.* Nashville, Tenn.: Thomas Nelson.

Halverstadt, J. 1998. *ADD and Romance.* Dallas, Tex.: Taylor Publishing Co.

Hartmann, T. 1998. *Healing ADD: Simple Exercises That Will Change Your Life.* Grass Valley, Calif.: Underwood Books.

Levin, F. R. 2000. Substance abuse and adult ADHD. *Psychiatric Times* 17(2).

Nadeau, K. G. 1996. *Adventures in Fast Forward: Life, Love, and Work for the ADD Adult.* New York: Brunner/Mazel Publishers.

Prager, D. 1998. *Happiness Is a Serious Problem: A Human Nature Repair Manual.* New York: Regan Books.

Roberts, M. S., and G. J. Jansen. 1997. *Living with ADD: A Workbook for Adults with Attention Deficit Disorder.* Oakland, Calif.: New Harbinger Publications.

Sudderth, D. B., and J. Kandel. 1997. *Adult ADD: The Complete Handbook.* Rocklin, Calif.: Prima Publishing.

Some Other
New Harbinger Titles

The Daughter's-In-Law Survival Guide, Item DSG $12.95

Whose Life Is It Anyway?, Item $14.95

It Happened to Me, Item IHPM $17.95

Act it Out, Item AIO $19.95

Parenting Your Older Adopted Child, Item PYAO $16.95

Boy Talk, Item BTLK $14.95

Talking to Alzheimer's, Item TTA $12.95

Helping a Child with Nonverbal Learning Disorder or Asperger's Syndrome, Item HCNL $14.95

The 50 Best Ways to Simplify Your Life, Item FWSL $11.95

When Anger Hurts Your Relationship, Item WARY $13.95

The Couple's Survival Workbook, Item CPSU $18.95

Loving Your Teenage Daughter, Item LYTD $14.95

The Hidden Feeling of Motherhood, Item HFM $14.95

Parenting Well When Your Depressed, Item PWWY $17.95

Thinking Pregnant, Item TKPG $13.95

Pregnancy Stories, Item PS $14.95

The Co-Parenting Survival Guide, Item CPSG $14.95

Family Guide to Emotional Wellness, Item FGEW $24.95

How to Survive and Thrive in an Empty Nest, Item NEST $13.95

Children of the Self-Absorbed, Item CSAB $14.95

The Adoption Reunion Survival Guide, Item ARSG $13.95

Undefended Love, Item UNLO $13.95

Why Can't I Be the Parent I Want to Be?, Item PRNT $12.95

Kid Cooperation, Item COOP $14.95

Breathing Room: Creating Space to Be a Couple, Item BR $14.95

Why Children Misbehave and What to do About it, Item BEHV $14.95

Couple Skills, Item SKIL $15.95

The Power of Two, Item PWR $15.95

Call **toll free, 1-800-748-6273,** or log on to our online bookstore at **www.newharbinger.com** to order. Have your Visa or Mastercard number ready. Or send a check for the titles you want to New Harbinger Publications, Inc., 5674 Shattuck Ave., Oakland, CA 94609. Include $4.50 for the first book and 75¢ for each additional book, to cover shipping and handling. (California residents please include appropriate sales tax.) Allow two to five weeks for delivery.

Prices subject to change without notice.